KINGDOM FINANCES FOR KINGDOM BUILDING

KELLIE L. MORGAN

Copyright © 2011 by Kellie L. Morgan

Kingdom Finances for Kingdom Building
by Kellie L. Morgan

Printed in the United States of America

ISBN 9781619044340

All rights reserved solely by the author. The author guarantees all contents are original and do not infringe upon the legal rights of any other person or work. No part of this book may be reproduced in any form without the permission of the author. The views expressed in this book are not necessarily those of the publisher.

Unless otherwise indicated, Bible quotations are taken from The Holy Bible, New International Version®, NIV®. Copyright © 1973, 1978, 1984 by International Bible Society; and The New King James Version. Copyright © 1982 by Thomas Nelson, Inc. Used by permission of Zondervan Publishing House.

www.xulonpress.com

CONTENTS

Foreword by Stephanie Bennett vii
Acknowledgements ix
My Heart's Desire xiii
Financial Prayer xix
Personal Testimony xv
Introduction xxi

Part One: Changing Your Mindset 27

Chapter One: Releasing the Debt Mentality 29
Chapter Two: It's All About the Kingdom 35

Part Two: Ears to Hear 43

Chapter Three: I Am Talking
       but are You Listening 45

Part Three: Establishing a Vision 55

Chapter Four: Finances with a Destiny 57
Chapter Five: Write the Vision 64
Chapter Six: Make the Vision Plain 70

Part Four: Stewardship vs. Ownership...... 77

Chapter Seven: Lessons from the Garden........79
Chapter Eight: Double or Nothing...................93

Part Five: Giving...................................... 103

Chapter Nine: Don't Block Your Blessings.....105
Chapter Ten: Two Fish, Five Loaves 112
Chapter Eleven: You Reap What You Sow......118

Part Six: Checkbook Management.......... 123

Chapter Twelve: Setting Order in
   Your Finances.......................................125

**Part Seven: Establishing a
   Savings Account............................ 133**

Chapter Thirteen: All Season Finances..........135
Chapter Fourteen: Who Moved the Cheese? ..140
Chapter Fifteen: Get Up, Pick Up and Walk...149
Chapter Sixteen: Goliath Must Die.................156
Chapter Seventeen: The Ant Mentality 163

**Part Eight: Wisdom and
   Encouragement.............................. 165**

Chapter Eighteen: A Mother's Wisdom 167
Chapter Nineteen: Just a Little
   Encouragement.....................................170

Final Remarks 173

FORWARD

Money can be a difficult thing to manage. People in this world are always trying to figure out how to get it, how to maintain it, and how to make more of it. This proves to be even more challenging for those of us who live by a higher standard – God's standard. There are many rules and regulations that govern this world and how we are to look at and manage our money. However, Kellie breaks into this discussion with the boldness of God's standard in regards to our finances. She guides us into a real conversation about what lies beneath our inability to get it together.

Too often, discussion around money and finances makes us cringe, but after reading this book, I believe each reader will come away with a changed perspective. I was personally challenged to look beyond the surface and really explore the issues behind my financial issues. I now find myself taking the necessary steps in surrendering my money to God and moving towards financial freedom. Kellie walks us through the journey as she exposes the spiritual chains that have our blessings held up.

Listen to the message of financial freedom in this book and hear Kellie's heart. She is passionate about both money and the kingdom of God. As a woman of integrity, her heart for helping in the manifestation of kingdom finances in the lives of God's people will leap off of each page and inspire you on to get it right. God can and will bring freedom to every aspect of your life, even your pocketbook. Kellie's testimony bears witness to it. Take notes, answer the questions honestly, pray the prayers, and receive the freedom Kellie speaks into your life.

Your financial freedom is on the way and God will be pleased!

Stephanie Bennett

ACKNOWLEDGMENTS

To my Lord and Savior Jesus Christ, You are the solid Rock on which my life stands. Now that I have You in my life, I can not imagine going one day or second without You. You are the essence of who I am. You are the air that I breathe. It is only through You that I move, live and have my being. I can never repay You for what You did for me on Calvary. It is why I even exist today. I thank You with all of my heart, mind, body and soul for choosing me before I ever chose You. I honor and praise You for giving me life and life more abundantly. Thank you Father for knowing the plans You have for me plans to prosper me and not to harm me, plans to give me hope and a future (Jeremiah 29:11). And thank You for raising me up for such a time as this.

I challenge those of you who are reading this book, who do not know God as your personal Lord and personal Savior. Give Him a try. He is real. He will never leave you nor forsake you, nor will He ever fail you. I have tried over and over again, but one thing I can honestly say is I haven't found a love that tops His. He is truly a Friend, Lover and Companion. Take the plunge by confessing with your mouth, Jesus is Lord, and believing in your heart God raised Him from the dead, you will be saved (Romans 10:9). I promise, the journey is worth taking and the ride is enjoyable. Your life will never be the same. Call to Him and He will answer you and tell you great and unsearchable things you do not know (Jeremiah 33:3).

To Mom and Dad, thanks for helping me become the person I am today. Dad, thanks for teaching me a mind is a terrible thing to waste. Mom, thanks for all your prayers, that alien turned out to be a beautiful butterfly. Thank you both for enduring the rough places with me, and believing in me when I did not believe in myself. Your love and support has been my wings. You are the GREATEST.

To my auntie, brothers, sister-in-law, niece, nephews, cousins and extended family, you are the BOMB!! And you keep me on my toes. I couldn't imagine life without you.

To Kita and Efrem, you are the best. Thanks for editing my book and believing in me. I don't know what I would have done without you. God bless you abundantly.

To Satrice, you are RADICAL!! Thanks for inspiring me, challenging me and reminding me that I can do all things through Christ who strengthens me. You showed up just in time. You are truly a woman of virtue, purpose and vision. Keep doing what you are doing and see you at the top. Can't wait to your music come out. You've got something to say and I am your number one fan. Thanks for being more than a friend, but an inspiration.

To Elder Marlise, thank you for your spiritual wisdom and prophetic words. You challenge me to be the best that I can be and to always stay close to Jesus Christ at the cost of being rejected. You are truly a woman of divine greatness. Thank you for being a true leader, who lives what she preaches.

To Bishop Joseph Warren Walker, III and the entire Mount Zion Family of Nashville, Tennessee, thanks for being my foundation and the solid rock on which I stand. Your spiritual foundation keeps pushing me higher. Thanks for being there when I needed you most and for keeping a watchful eye over me as I continue along this journey. You will always be home, no matter where I go. I love you with an everlasting love.

To Apostles Michael and Lorelle Rich and the entire Royal Life Family for challenging, supporting and encouraging me to birth the seven-week financial empowerment course which ultimately led to this book and a peace of my destiny. Thank you for seeing the gifts inside of me and having the courage to pull them out. Apostle Michael, I am determined to live the incredible life. Prophetess Lorelle, I didn't miss the destiny call. You both have impacted my life forever and I bless the day you entered my life.

To Stephanie Bennette, thanks for doing the final edits and writing my forward. God knew I needed you for such a time as this. Thanks for showing up. Know that your gifts are valuable to the kingdom and you are a force to be reckoned with. Thanks for inspiring and motivating me to complete this project, as well as being midwife to help push this baby out.

Last, but definitely not least, to Sandy Powell and the entire Powerhouse Ministry Team, thank you for being the prophetic voices in my life. Thanks helping me to stand strong on the promises of the Lord, while in waiting. I can't wait to hear your voices reign throughout the earth. My life is truly the evidence of your fruit.

MY HEART'S DESIRE

It is my heart's desire to see us, the people of God, live life and life more abundantly in every aspect of our lives, especially in our finances. Financial bondage keeps us from fulfilling God's commission to spread the gospel to the four corners of the earth. It is time for the people of God to be loosed in their finances and not be confined to the things of this world. "Now it shall come to pass, if you diligently obey the voice of the LORD your God, to observe carefully all His commandments which I command you today, the LORD your God will set you high above all nations of the earth (Deuteronomy 28:1, NKJV)." God's word does not return unto Him void. If He said it, it will come to pass. Our part is to be obedient to His plan for our lives in order to reap the financial prosperity necessary for encouraging, edifying, exhorting and building of His kingdom.

I believe there is power in numbers and we as a body must come together as one force to transform this earth, this country, this people and the nations. Imagine if we all surrendered our finances back to the Lord and gathered on one accord in our giving just like they did in Acts

19:17-20, then the word of the Lord will spread widely and grow in power. Then we will experience the financial miracles we have been expecting in our lives and others.

It is my heart's desire for our finances as a people to become finances that build and support the purposes of the Lord. Take this challenge with me and I promise God will show us great and unsearchable things we have never known (Jeremiah 33:3, NIV).

PERSONAL TESTIMONY

Monday, November 28, 2005, I came home to begin my second day of writing this book. Much to my dismay, the computer containing the book was fried. I couldn't understand what was going on since I had a surge protector and nothing else on the plug was destroyed. The computer had my book on it. Fortunately, I had saved it on a disk. Praise the Lord for His divine protection.

This was more evidence that I was destined to write this book for this season. Not only was I fighting to complete this book, but I was fighting for my financial freedom also. I have never experienced such warfare trying to get anything done. The Spirit of the Lord came upon me and I began to declare the word of the Lord over my circumstance.

Now faith is the substance of things hoped for, the evidence of things not seen (Hebrews 11:1, NKJV). God will supply all of my needs, according to His riches and glory (Philippians 4:19, NKJV). God is with me so whom shall I fear. He will make me to lie down in green pastures. It is not by my might, nor by my power (Zechariah 4:6), but by the Spirit of the Lord that I will complete this race that has been set before me. God will not put more on me than I can bear, so I can complete this book.

I am thrilled today because this is the day God has wiped the dirt from my spiritual eyes and revealed another portion of my destiny and purpose. I was born to do this, and I will walk in the fullness of this promise. Scripture tells us, "The thief comes only to steal, kill and destroy (John 10:10)." Now, I realize he will never come after something that doesn't glorify God. But with my faith in God, he can not kill my destiny. He can only cause turbulence, which will only propel me to higher heights.

"When the enemy comes in like a flood, The Spirit of the LORD will lift up a standard against him (Isaiah 59:19, NKJV)." Indeed the Spirit of the LORD lifted up a standard against him and gave me a determination to get this book done. It was by any means necessary, whether it meant I had to write the book by hand, or go out and buy another computer in the midst of trying to get out of debt.

One thing I am learning in this process, destiny is about sacrifice. It is about being determined to do what God has called me to do, at any cost. I can't wait to see what God will do in our lives through this book. Destiny does not stop because of obstacles, hindrances, situations, and circumstances, but it pushes one to use those things to rise above and soar to heights never seen before.

Like an eagle that uses the storms to soar to higher heights, I am ready to fly to my optimum range of sight and see things I have never seen before in Christ Jesus. This is going to be a wonderful journey for us all and I can't wait to see the end of our story. I am also on my way to debt freedom and I am enjoying the ride to kingdom finances that will build the kingdom of God. However, the information contained in this book is my own personal experiences or divine inspirations given by God while journeying this road to debt freedom. I think the one unique factor about this book is we get to walk this journey out with you. How awesome is that. We can grow, achieve, laugh, cry and smile together. Who knows, there might be a part two.

MY FINANCIAL PRAYER FOR YOU

I pray as you read this book God will show you great and unsearchable things you did not know concerning your finances. He will open up the windows of heaven and pour you out a blessing you do not have room enough to receive. I pray as God prospers you in your finances, and gives you seed along the way, you will sow back into His kingdom. Your mind will be transformed and renewed concerning your finances as you open up the word of God and discover His financial treasures for your life. You will see the impossible, miraculous, and unexpected show up in your finances as you position them to build the kingdom of God.

I decree and declare over your life, you are the head and not the tail, you are above and not beneath, you are a lender and not a borrower because God has called you to be a royal priesthood, a chosen generation and a holy nation. You are obedient to the Lord; therefore, He will restore unto you the years the locusts have eaten. Because you are faithful in your giving, He is giving you greater seed to sow. You are fruitful, multiplying, ruling, reigning and having dominion on this earth. The promises of God have already been established in heaven on your behalf and they shall manifest on this earth. You are ordained to be a blessing upon this earth, so everything that you release upon this earth and into the lives of others will come back to you pressed down, shaking together and running over in your life. I pray these blessing upon you, your house and your finances, in Jesus Christ name. AMEN

INTRODUCTION

Kingdom Finances for Kingdom building was initially a seven-week financial empowerment course that was birthed at Royal Life International Ministries in July 2005. It began as a charge to me by Prophetess Lorelle to write a financial empowerment ministry, as a result of the people crying out for help with their finances. I have to be honest and say that I did not see it in myself, and typically when I am not sure of myself, I begin to procrastinate, but thanks to Prophetess that she did not give up on me. She pushed me, and like any loving mother who sees the potential in their child, she put the fire under my tale and gave me a deadline date. Only God could have told her to do that since I am big on deadline dates. Despite me, God was faithful and I was given the opportunity, not only to birth a ministry, but publicly teach the seven week financial course, Kingdom Finances for Kingdom Building.

This God ordained season taught me so much about the spiritual gifts that reside on the inside of me. It helped me to step out of my shyness, but to also trust what I was hearing from the Lord. It brought a greater revelation of my ministry call scripture: Isaiah 61. Being called to the deliverance ministry for me is not just about setting people free from demonic spirits, but it is setting people free financially by evoking, empowering and encouraging them to take a financial stance with the word of God, by listening to the Holy Spirit and doing the natural things they know to do.

God showed me that if I would surrender all my gifts whether natural or spiritual to Him, then He could put His super on my natural and merge the two. I am naturally gifted with finances. Finances have been my passion since I was a little girl. After accepting my call to ministry, I never knew how the Lord would use this gift with my ministry call, but it was during this season, He fused the two and brought forth the greater revelation.

I like Joseph can teach others how to make it through a financial famine and walk with them through that season. Proverbs 18:16 says, "A man's gifts will make room for him, and bring him before great men." This season not only made room for my gifts, but it brought me before great men. It also set me up for where I am now in my life, writing this book titled, Kingdom Finances for Kingdom Building. This season of my life brought so many valuable lessons, but it also helped me to understand how God will use the very things that I struggle with and use them to bless others.

I remember being in the first grade and my teacher telling my mother I was slow and needed to be put in remedial courses because I was not up to speed with the other children. She told my mother I was incapable of learning and would not amount to very much in life. Every report card I received had N's, which meant needs improvement. In addition to labeling me slow, this teacher would compare me to my older brother. My brother is the extrovert, and I am the introvert. He is more of the performer, whereas, I am more the analytical type. I guess this is why we both chose the careers we chose. He is an Engineer and I am an Accountant. We are radically different and do not learn things the same way. The teacher never wanted to get to know me as a student. She wanted me to perform like my brother.

Today, I understand it was not the teacher who was labeling me, but it was the enemy attacking my destiny. He was planting seeds of doubt, inferiority, low-self esteem and competition within me. I had to deal with this throughout my elementary years because I would always end up with the teachers who taught my older brother. They would always compare me to him. But one thing I can say, "God always had my back, and He will have yours too. There is a purpose and plan for everything both you and I will encounter in life. Nothing happens by accident or coincidence, absolutely nothing."

Despite what the teachers were saying, my mother was not having it. She stood up for me and refused to listen to the teachers. She told them they were not putting her child in any special education classes, and to stop comparing me to my brother because both of her children were different. My mother always said, my brother is more like the hare/rabbit, and I was more like the turtle in life.

Most people who know me would not ever guess that I am very shy and withdrawn. I will sit back and quietly assess a situation before I will interact with someone or attempt a task. I guess you can call me a perfectionist. I am also stubborn, so you pretty much can't get me to do things I do not want to do. Hey God is working on me. I think my stubbornness and shyness had more to do with my grades than intelligence. I am very smart, but I guess when you are not the life of the party then most people label you weird or dumb.

God sent me an angel when I got to the second grade. This teacher was different, even though she also had my brother for a student. Mrs. Grizzwald was her name. She was an awesome teacher because she took the time out to learn how each of her students learned. She just didn't throw subject matter at you; she wanted you to understand it. I think she figured out early on that I was nothing like my brother. When she would ask me to read in front of the other children, I would not do so well, but when she would ask me to read one on one with her, I would do just fine. She noticed I was shy and told my mother to give me a little time to come into my own. She also recommended my mother get me tutors and make sure I did everything out loud. My reading began to improve, but I was still struggling with math, especially those times-tables.

My mother tried everything to help me with math. She got cue cards. She hired a tutor. She was down to her last. But the answer was in the house. My father was really good at math, but he was the last person who would want to teach you anything. He was very impatient. I remember the night she said, "I can't take this anymore, you are just going to have to go in there with your daddy and let him help you with your math homework." I knew I was in trouble then.

I went and got on the bed and asked my father to help. I thought I would not ever make it through that first assignment because any time I would stop to think about doing the problem, my father would pop my hands and shout, "Stop thinking and do that problem. I am not going to be here all night with you. You know what you are doing, just do it." Then he would say, "Shon, the mind is a terrible thing to waste." You might think what a harsh way to learn, but I was learning more than a math lesson. I was learning confidence.

Today, I thank God for that experience with my father because I gained the confidence I needed to be successful not only in math, but in life by not second guessing my self and doing what I know to do. That experience also taught me that procrastination is something that I have to overcome. I realize today that I was a perfectionist. If I didn't think I was going to get the answer right, then I didn't want to do it. From that day forward, my confidence was built and math became my favorite subject. In fact, I became an honor roll student from second grade until the day I graduated from high school.

It was also in elementary school where I decided I wanted to be an accountant. In 1995, my dream manifested, I got a degree in Accounting from Middle Tennessee State University. You can't tell me life and death is not in the power of your tongue (Proverbs 18:21). You have what you speak. But also God knows the plans He has for your life. They are plans to prosper you, not to harm you, but to give you a hope and a future (Jeremiah 29:11). And what God has planned for your life, no demon or devil in hell can stop it from manifesting in your life, and neither can you.

At an early age, I discovered I was really good with money. My parents would give us an allowance every week. I always had money because I would save. My brother on the other hand was the total opposite. I remember saving about twenty-five dollars and my mother took us to the mall. I refused to buy anything for myself, but my brother was on one of his spending rampages. He wanted to buy some sea monkeys, but didn't have enough money. For some reason, I allowed my brother to talk me into helping him buy those sea monkeys, which were nothing more than floating little bacteria and basically, a waste of my money. Looking back, this was my first investment lesson. The awesome thing is at least I didn't spend all of my money. Needless to say, this would not be the last time I would learn a financial lesson from a family member.

PART ONE

Changing Your Mindset

Chapter One

RELEASING THE DEBT MENTALITY

❦

Romans 12:2 - *"Do not conform any longer to the pattern of this world, but be transformed by the renewing of your mind. Then you will be able to test and approve what God's will is, His good, pleasing and perfect will (NIV)."*

I remember when I first began to establish a relationship with Jesus; there were things in my life that I knew I could no longer hold onto, like cursing. I came from a family of cursers. And as we know, generational curses flow down to the fourth generations. I needed help because cursing came natural to me. I needed the Lord to change my language. I needed a new vocabulary, something else to proclaim. So I asked the Lord to give me a scripture that dealt with cursing.

God is such a romancer. He will use uncommon ways to get you to fall in love with him, like playing Russian roulette with you. This is when you are going through something or have questions, and you open your bible and it falls on a scripture that is just what you needed to hear. However, you soon find out, this season is not forever. It ends rather quickly.

Well, I opened my bible and it fell on James Chapter 3, "Taming the Tongue." I was amazed because God had answered my prayer. Everyday, I would read James chapter 3 because I wanted to really understand what it was saying, plus I wanted to memorize the scripture. At the time, I didn't know anything about getting the word in my spirit. I just knew I needed something else to say instead of profanity. I needed a word to remind me not to curse.

Anytime I would think about cursing, I would say, "Fresh water and salt water can not flow from the same spring." After about a month of this, my cursing had almost diminished. Today, my language has totally changed as a result of the word of God in my life. Without knowing it, I had followed the principles Paul gave us in Romans 12:2. I had allowed the word of God to transform me by renewing my mind, words and thoughts. It was no longer acceptable for me to curse or even listen to others curse around me. I discovered God's good, perfect and acceptable will for my life. My mouth was created to bless, instead of curse, and to proclaim the good news of Jesus Christ.

Just as I did with cursing, we can do this with any area of our lives, especially finances. Do you know many of us are in debt because of generational curses over our lives? Generational curses are sins, iniquities and transgressions that have been passed down to the fourth generation, and even word curses spoken over a generation of people (Deuteronomy 5:8-10).

An example of a generational curse is when you see poverty running from one generation to another generation in your family. It seems no one can ever get ahead in your family. Mama was on welfare, the children are on welfare and the children's children are on welfare. Someone has to repent for the sins of the forefathers to break the generation curse off the family line. Someone has to decide to do something different instead of accepting what has been, and not feel guilty for wanting more and better.

An example of word curses is when someone says, "You are not ever going to have anything because your mother did not have anything and your daddy did not have anything." Another example could be someone simply telling you, "You are always going to owe somebody something."

You do not have to accept those words for your life. It is very possible to live a debt free life. There are people on this earth living it, and they did not come from wealth, nor did they hit the lottery. Our responsibility is to apply the word of God and seek the knowledge, Godly counsel and wisdom of those who are living the debt free life. "Blessed is the man who walks not in the counsel of the ungodly, nor stand in the path of sinners, nor sits in the seat of the scornful; but his delight is in the law of the Lord, and in His law he meditates day and night (Psalms 1:1-2)."

Another reason people are in debt is because they have not dealt with issues or things that happened to them in their childhood. Therefore, they overcompensate to fill voids in their life with things. This is idolatry. God wants us to lean and depend on Him for everything. He is the only One who can complete you and fill every void in your life. We are to worship the Creator, not the creation. I am not against having nice things. However, nothing in our life is to take the place of God. He is a jealous God. This is why many people who are wealthy are miserable. Somewhere along the way, their worship became perverted. They began to worship things, money and success, instead of worshipping God or they became the worshipped, instead of giving the glory to God.

Debt freedom begins in your mind. You must be willing to replace the lies you have believed about money and your ability to be a steward over it with the truth. The truth can be found in the word of God. Just as I stated above, find out what God has to say, and begin to apply it to your life. Do not just be a hearer of the word, but be a doer of the word (James 1:22-23). Work the word and it will work for you. Remember, the race is not given to the swift, so keep pushing until you meet your expected end. Unless you hit the lottery or receive an inheritance, getting out of debt is a process. It does not happen overnight. But with time, discipline, patience and wisdom, you can live a debt free life.

EXERCISE – CHAPTER 1

1. What generational curse is running through your family?
   _____
   _____
   _____

2. What mindset/lie do you need to change about money?
   _____
   _____
   _____

3. What does God have to say about what you believe? Find a scripture you can hold in your heart and bring to remembrance.
   _____
   _____
   _____

4. Name someone around you who know is living a debt free life? Ask that person how they became debt free.
   _____
   _____
   _____

PRAYER AND DECLARATION

Dear Heavenly Father, I realize I have a false belief about money and finances. I surrender my thoughts, beliefs, values and behaviors regarding finances to you. I am asking you to come into my heart and reveal your truth to me. Now lead, guide and direct me into all truth and set me free from this financial bondage. Make the crooked places straight. Break the curses that are holding me bound. Show me your truth and light up the pathway of righteousness so I can see the destiny and purpose you have for me.

I decree and declare over my life, I am laying aside every weight and sin that so easily besets me. I am a lender not a borrower. I am the head and not the tail. I have the mind of Christ and I am walking in freedom and liberty in every area of my life. AMEN.

Chapter Two

IT'S ALL ABOUT THE KINGDOM

***

Matthew 6:10 - *"Thy kingdom come, Thy will be done on earth as it is in heaven (KJV)."*

As I sit here and meditate upon this scripture, I am overwhelmed by the power of Jesus Christ and all of His revelation. I couldn't imagine how this scripture of text would speak to me about finances. The Lord quickly reminded me of a song I love on the Shekinah Glory Live CD by Kingdom Valley Ministries titled, *"It's all about the Kingdom."* By the way, if you are a fan of worship music, and want to go to the next dimension of God, this would be the CD to do it. In fact, I recommend anything they produce, ahhhh the glory. Sorry but I got caught up right there just thinking about the worship.

Alright, back to how this scripture brought revelation to me about finances. I realized Jesus was all about His Father's business, which was the kingdom. So, I looked up the word "kingdom" in the American Heritage College dictionary. I chose two of the definitions to make my point: (1) the eternal spiritual sovereignty of God or Christ and (2) A realm or sphere in which one thing is dominant.[1]

The Nelson's New Illustrated Bible Dictionary defines kingdom as a "state or nation with a form of government in which a king or queen serves as supreme ruler."[2] So with that being said, the kingdom is a nation where God, our Lord and Savior Jesus Christ is the King. He is the ruler, the One who is in control of everything and owns everything. He is the supreme ruler; therefore, everything is under His feet. And everything under Him must submit to His authority and sovereignty, even money. If you believe this you will submit to the principles, statutes and commandments God has given you in His holy Word concerning money.

Everything we do must be done with a kingdom mindset. The kingdom of God operates between two extremes, the spirit and the natural. This reminds me of the Lord's Prayer, "Thy kingdom come, Thy will be done on earth as it already is in heaven (Matthew 6:10, KJV)." We as believers have the ability to bring heaven down to earth, especially when we operate in the principles of God, which is His way of doing things. In order to achieve this, we can not be led by our flesh, but we must be led by the Spirit of the Lord because God has a way of doing things that doesn't make sense to the natural man.

The word tells us, "The man without the Spirit does not accept the things that come from the

Spirit of God, for they are foolishness to him, and he cannot understand them, because they are spiritually discerned (1 Corinthians 2:14)." However, God will use the foolish things to shame the wise (1 Corinthians 1:27). Example: Does it make sense to pay tithes when your bills are piled high? The answer is "No" in the natural, but "Yes" in the spirit. God's economy does not work like the world's economy and I am a living witness to this. Since I began paying tithes I have seen God do some crazy, unattainable things with my finances.

I always live beyond what I make using God's economic system of operation. This is different than living beyond your means with the world's economy. I am talking about when you are down to your last and God's manna shows up in your circumstance (Exodus 16:15-18). In biblical scripture, manna means, "What is this?" However, manna to me is God's unexpected provision that flows into your situation right when you need it from an unexpected source. This leads me to another testimony.

I got paid on Friday, December 11, 2006. After plugging my tithes and estimated bills into my budget, I was supposed to have exactly nine dollars and thirty-one cent ($9.31) left. On paper and in the natural, I had $9.31, but in the spirit realm, I had more than enough. God's hand moved upon my circumstance and turned the water into wine.

My first reaction was to get depressed, but my spirit said, "No. I will praise the Lord at all times. God is a Promise Keeper. He is Jehovah Jireh, My Provider. He will do just what He said. He promised if I was faithful to pay tithes and offering, He would open the windows of heaven and pour me out a blessing that I would not have room enough to receive (Malachi 3:10). He would supply all of my needs according to His riches and glory (Philippians 4:19, NKJV). And whatever state I am in, I am still blessed."

I got a song in my heart and began to sing right there at my desk. I began to praise God because all of my bills were paid, I had food in the refrigerator, clothes on my back and I had $9.31, an amount that most people on the street wished they had. When I praised, God began to work because I got an e-mail telling me our longevity checks would be posted to our accounts on the following Tuesday and a couple of my bills were not as much as I thought they were going to be. After God finished working on my behalf, I had almost $80.00. Now this is what I am talking about, living beyond what you make. God's economy turned $9.31 into $80.00 in just a matter of minutes. Can you say with me? Trust God!!!

Again I say, "Kingdom economy does not work like the world's economy." The world tells you two plus two equals four, but the kingdom might say two plus two equals one hundred or one thousand. The world tells you that you have to buy a house, but the kingdom tells you, "God will give you houses you did not build." The kingdom will say, "Sow a seed to help someone else get out of debt, while you are in debt or sow a seed into someone's life that is mortgage free, so you can be mortgage free." But remember, in whatever you do, make sure that you are being led by the Spirit and not your flesh.

I want to encourage you, God is an unlimited God. He can do whatever He wants to do. He has the power to make the impossible come to pass. Do not put Him in a box. His blessing might not come how you want it to come or even look the way you want it to look. But whatever you do, please do not compare yourself with someone else. What works for someone else might not work for you. Just flow with the Spirit and watch the Lord do exceedingly, abundantly, above and beyond what you can ever think or imagine (Ephesians 3:20, NKJV).

I dare not leave this chapter without saying again, "It is all about the Kingdom." I am not encouraging you to get out of debt for you, but to get out of debt to be a blessing to the kingdom of God. We have a mandate as Christians to spread the gospel of Jesus Christ, to help the poor, the sick and the widowed. It would be such a blessing if you could help someone else become debt free.

Here is an example to encourage you. I was watching a service of Bishop Eddie Long on television. During the service a young lady laid her credit cards at the altar. Bishop Long, asked, "Who laid the card at the altar?" When the girl came forth, He paid the card off for her. I am not talking about paying a payment, but he paid the entire balance to get her out of debt. I think what blessed me the most was he was preaching about something totally different, but followed the Spirit. Many people were freed from debt because Bishop Long followed the Spirit and his example encouraged others who were financially free, to sow to release others into financial freedom.

How many times have you wanted to help someone less fortunate than you, but couldn't because you are tangled up in financial bondage? I tell you, it is not a good feeling. I want us to be free to live the abundant life, not for ourselves, but for the glory of the Lord. So let's ride and give the devil a black eye.

ENDNOTES

1. *The American Heritage Dictionary,* Third Edition. Boston: Houghton Mifflin Company, 1993, p. 748.

2. Youngblood, R.F; Bruce, F.F & Harrison, R.K, *New Illustrated Bible Dictionary,* Nashville, Tennessee: Thomas Nelson Publishers, 1995, 1986, p. 728.

EXERCISE – CHAPTER 2

1. **How is the kingdom manifesting in your financial life?**
   _____
   _____
   _____
   _____

2. **Remember a time when God showed up in your finances?**
   _____
   _____
   _____
   _____

3. **Name an area in your finances where you are not manifesting the kingdom and ask God to show you the truth in His Word.**
   _____
   _____
   _____
   _____

4. **Pray and ask God to lay someone on your heart to sow a seed into their life.**
   _____
   _____
   _____
   _____

PRAYER AND DECLARATION

Dear Heavenly Father, I reverence you as my Lord and King. You are a sovereign God. Everything in this earth belongs to you, so I submit myself and everything you have entrusted to me under your authority. Just as you were about your Father's business, so will I be about your business and bring forth your glory on this earth with everything you have allowed to be within my stewardship. In the areas I am obedient, Father bless me and make me a ruler over much. In the areas where I am being disobedient, Father I repent and ask you to shape me, mold me and transform me into your holiness and righteousness. Show me your truth and I will hide it within my heart. I promise to diligently obey you because I know it is your desire for me to be fruitful and to multiply, but most of all to be blessed and to be a blessing. I decree and declare over my life, I am the righteousness of God. He created me in His image and likeness so I have nothing to worry about. All my needs are met; therefore, nothing is missing, lacking or broken in my life, so I can release and let go. I was born to be a blessing, so I will be a conduit to bless others all over this world. I am about my Father's business and I will bring glory to His name in all that I have in my possession. AMEN.

PART TWO

EARS TO HEAR

Chapter Three

I AM TALKING, BUT ARE YOU LISTENING?

Psalm 116:1-2 - *"I love the Lord, for He heard my voice; He heard my cry for mercy. Because He turned His ear to me, I will call on Him as long as I live (NIV)."*

I love this passage of scripture because it expresses the power of having a voice, as well as, the importance of being heard. Everyday people go through life trying to be heard, whether it is through the clothing they wear, the car they drive, and nowadays, the church they attend. People just want to know someone cares about what they are saying, whether they are talking or not. I know you are saying, "What is she talking about?"

Well, typically when I am upset about something, I will do either one of two things: I will be silent or I will speak up. To be honest, my silence is often more powerful than my words. This is why I have a tendency to retreat to myself when I am upset, so I will not say things based on my emotions. I was taught if you do not have something good to say, then do not say anything at all. However, I am not good at internalizing things. Usually, I have to let it out and then I am good to go. The point is this, whether I am vocal or silent, I am voicing my opinion.

What is important to me is whether someone heard me, and if they are willing to do something about what they heard me say. This is why I love this scripture so much because David, the psalmist, was expressing himself to the Lord whether it was through his voice or through his tears and God heard him and did something about what He heard.

I will never forget the 1996 Presidential Election. There was mass marketing for everyone to register to vote. It was important for every voice to be heard, because one voice could impact the decision of who would win the election.

Prior to that election, I was one of those voices that were never heard at the polls. My attitude was there are two devils and you tell me I have to vote for one of them? Voting was like saying, "I know you are both devils, now tell me which one of you is going to be a little less devilish than the other." I know, I know, I know, I had the wrong attitude and I bore no thought to the historical plight behind my right to vote. All I knew was that I was not voting for the better of the two devils, and I stood firmly on that wrong philosophy. However, something was different about the 1996 election. Something took over me and I felt compelled to vote. Today, I know it was the

Holy Spirit. Knowing my voice could make a difference, encouraged and empowered me to register to vote.

My mindset changed from worrying about voting for the lesser of two evils to the knowledge that my voice has power. My voice had the power to decide who the next President would be. I knew if my opinion was voiced, then someone was bound to listen and do something about what I was saying with my vote. In the end, Bill Clinton and Al Gore were elected for a second term. This was the second time in history that a Democratic ticket was elected to office for a second term. I was astonished at the thought that my voice could have influenced the election and the manifestation of this history making event.

Now, what does this have to do with money? Well to tell you the truth, it has a lot to do with it. Believe it or not, your money has a voice. It has been talking to you for a long time, whether you have been listening or not. I don't know what your money has been saying to you. But if you find yourself busted, disgusted and discouraged with your finances, I guarantee you your money is telling you, "You are not making wise decisions." Now please do not get this confused with life. Sometimes in life things happen that we cannot control. But, I am talking about those things, which you have been doing out of your flesh, causing you to sink deeper into debt.

For example, you are grocery shopping. You've gotten everything on your list, and you are ready to check out. Much to your surprise there is a line. You are hungry and the children are screaming for candy and cokes. To get the children to calm down, you cave in to what they want. You start grabbing candy bars and drinks for the children. You see a magazine about your favorite star or how to loose twenty pounds in two weeks, so you get it. Before you know it, you have just added ten dollars or more to your grocery budget and the store has accomplished what it has set out to do, getting you to spend more money than you planned.

Believe it or not, the stores purposely set things you will not ordinarily buy at the register because this is the last chance they have to increase their sales. Plus they know you are going to grab that magazine because there is a wait in line. And this society tells us to always be doing something. They have the candy and drinks there because they know your children are going to be with you. The first time they set their eyes on that candy and you say, "No," they will get to hollering, crying and screaming. You will buy it just to shut them up. Yes I know, you don't think the candy, drinks, and magazine is a lot. Trust me, enough of these unplanned purchases could add up to an establishment of a savings account or emergency fund. They could even be the extra ten or twenty dollars you could put towards getting yourself out of debt. So again, I ask you, "What is your money saying to you and are you willing to hear it?"

I know there are some readers that are saying, "My money isn't saying that to me. I have a savings account, a 401k and an emergency fund, and I am not in debt." Well are you paying your tithes and offering to your local church? Are you using the surplus God has given you to build His kingdom, or helping someone else get financial freedom? If you are not doing any of these things, then you are hoarding money.

God does not bless us to be a blessing to ourselves, but to be a blessing to others. I am sure if you are not following the principles of God, you are loosing surplus somewhere. I am sure something unexpected dealing with money is always happening in your life. Yes, you always have the money in your hands to pay for it, but you are missing the point. If you don't voluntarily sow into God's kingdom, He will find a way to do it for you. However, you will not reap the benefits and interest it would have brought to you if you had done it for yourself.

Example, God has laid it on your heart to sow one hundred dollars into someone's life. You make the decision not to do it because you need the money to go on vacation. The next week, you are on your way to your vacation spot. While on the highway, you have a flat tire. Not only do you have to pay for a new tire, but you also have to pay for a tow truck to come get you. Yes, maybe this does not cancel your trip, but you have spent a hundred or more dollars. Just maybe God was trying to get you to release the seed to prevent the flat tire. So I challenge you to think about someone other than yourself, if you got it going on. Listen to the Lord and listen to what your money is saying to you. You might find out that you are selfish, self-centered and inconsiderate. But there is hope if you are willing to change.

Money matters are just like flies. They will buzz in your ear, until you get frustrated enough to pay attention. You can choose to swat them away, but they are going to come back. You can run, duck and dive, but like a track runner with a second-wind; they will catch up with you. Stop running from your money matters and choose to see things differently by first changing your attitude. Secondly, listen to what your money is saying about you and to you. It will help you change your life. But in the same sense, don't allow it to rule you. You should be ruling it according to the principles of God. Remember, God gave you dominion, power and authority to rule over everything on this earth.

God never intended for His people to be ruled by anything. It was His original intent that you rule, reign and have dominion over everything on this earth because He could trust you with the principles, laws and commandments He set and put into your spirit man. He wanted you to be successful and live an abundant life. He gave you the tools to do so through His word. Trust me, His principles work. We as believers have to use them if we are going to be successful in the eyes of God and not man.

There are many in this world we deem to be successful. However, in God's eyes they are failures because they are not following His principles. Hebrews 12:26-27 says, "Yet once more I shake not only the earth, but also heaven." Now this, yet once more, indicates the removal of those things that are being shaken, as of things that are made, that then things which cannot be shaken may remain (NKJV)." You have a choice to do it God's way or do it your way, but know what you build will be shaken away, but what God builds will remain. You can have temporal prosperity or eternal prosperity, but you are going to have to release something. God's kingdom will cost you something. It is called sacrifice and surrender. Surrender your thoughts, behaviors, actions and attitudes unto the Lord. Change your mindset with the word of God. Open your ears to hear the word, the truth and watch God change your vision and your life.

EXERCISE – CHAPTER 3

1. Take a look at your environment (closets, drawers, cabinets, etc.) what is it telling you about your finances?
   _____
   _____
   _____

2. Do you need to make a change? If so what are you going to do about it? If not, what is holding you back or what could you being doing better?
   _____
   _____
   _____

3. Name some one you have helped financially in the last month? Is there something in your house/wallet that you need to release?
   _____
   _____
   _____

4. Get quiet, pray and ask the Lord to show you what He wants you to do with your finances.
   _____
   _____
   _____

PRAYER AND DECLARATION

Dear Father God, your Spirit dwells within me to lead, guide and direct me into all truth. The Spirit speaks your will to me and puts me on the straight and narrow path. Thank you, Father, for allowing me to hear your voice and not to follow a stranger. It is your desire that I prosper in everything I do, even in my finances. Father, show me the plan you have for me financially. Help me to take inventory of the things within my environment so I can release the things that I need to release and change the things I need to change financially. Guide me in my daily transactions and let them be for your glory. My greatest desire is to always listen and hear you when you say yes, no or not yet. I want to know your good, acceptable and perfect will is for my life and the finances you have released into my life.

I decree and declare over my life, I am your sheep, I hear your voice; therefore, I will not follow my flesh, will or even the voices of others. God you are Lord, Ruler over all, so again I surrender my daily transactions to you. I have faith, which means I am a hearer and a doer of your word. There isn't anything that I can't achieve in this life. I am a master over those things which you have given me dominion over and they will not master me because I am determined to serve you mentally, spiritually, emotionally, socially and financially. Father, help me to be a success financially so I can build your kingdom. AMEN

PART THREE
ESTABLISHING THE VISION

Chapter Four

FINANCES WITH A DESTINY

Proverbs 29:18 - *"Where there is no vision, the people perish, but he that keeps the law, happy is he (KJV)."*

I'd like to start this section off by asking you a question, "Would you get on an airplane without knowing where you were going? Would you go on a trip without knowing how you are going to get to your destination?" If I am correct, the answer to these questions is "No."

Many of us are planners, unless you are the bold and brave. We know our destination, how long it will take to get there, what we need to take on the trip and how we are going to get there. If we don't know how to get there and how long it will take, we will map quest our destination for directions and the estimated time of arrival. We will follow those directions without taking any detours. If you are in agreement with me, say, "Amen."

Well if this is true for you when traveling, then why is it so easy to start traveling down a financial journey without a vision or plan? Just as it is with traveling, if you don't know where you are going, how long it will take to get there, what you need on the trip and how you are going to get there, it will cost you dearly. This is how many of us get into financial trouble, so we end up on the road to bankruptcy, living from paycheck to paycheck, or not knowing where our money went. I am not talking about life happening. I am talking about not being a good steward and having a vision for your finances. You will perish without your financial road map.

When life throws you a financial blow, the best way to beat it is to get back up and keep moving. First and foremost, keep yourself built up in the word of God. Find out what His plan is for your life during this time. Don't allow yourself to be idle because it is the devil's play ground. Secondly, do what you have to do to generate income, morally and right. If this means you have to take something less than where you were to make it, then do it. If you have to work a couple of jobs, then do it or take advantage of the situation and create a business based upon your gifts and talents. How you look at the situation is all about your perception. Later on, I will tell you a little bit about my testimony of leaving a position to find my greater peace. The one thing that saved me during this time period was God's preparation to save almost a year's savings during what I call the glory days. But I didn't want to live off my savings or deplete them, so I took a job substitute teaching, mind you this was making five (5) percent of what I use to make. In other words, a drastic pay cut, but God blessed me and provided for me during this time. I had an opportunity to experience a summer in the midst of a season that should have been a winter.

Let's revisit the story about the sea monkeys. Remember, I told you, I was the saver and my brother was the spender. Whatever he wanted, he bought it. When he didn't have enough money, he would borrow it or find some other means of getting what he wanted. Typically, I was the means to his end. He would talk me into helping him and since I did not have a vision for my finances, I was vulnerable to his wants and desires. If I had a financial vision for my money, I would be telling you a different story today.

Well, maybe you didn't buy sea monkeys, but you went out to dinner or shopping with a friend, when you couldn't afford it. Maybe you told yourself, "I work everyday, I deserve a shopping spree." Before you knew it, the bill money was gone or you created another five hundred dollars of credit card debt. Now the bills are rolling in and you are robbing Peter to pay Paul. And your friend is nowhere to be found. Here is the reality. It took you just a few minutes to accumulate the debt, but it will take you years to get out of it.

One bad decision has cost you hundreds of dollars in late fees, interest, insufficient fund charges, and the embarrassment of borrowing money or the need to make payment arrangements. If you are honest with yourself, you are still paying the price for bad financial decisions you made years ago, whether it is bad credit or credit card debt. I don't want to discourage you because there is hope for your future. However, you are going to have to get focused and make quality decisions by establishing a financial vision. Then and only then will you begin to change your financial future.

What does it mean to have a vision? According to dictionary.com, "Vision is something that is or has been seen; the act or power of seeing; the special sense by which the qualities of an object (as color, luminosity, shape and size) constituting its appearance are perceived and which is meditated by the eye; and a vivid mental image."[1] In essence you have to be able to perceive and meditate with your eyes or get a vivid mental image of where you are going financially and what you are aiming towards financially.

For example, it is July and you want to pay off three credit cards before January. Your strategy is to pay the three smallest balances. You can accomplish your goal by paying an additional one hundred dollars ($100.00) to the minimum payment. Now get a vivid, intense picture in your mind of you paying the last credit card in December, and shouting I achieved my goal! Literally live, breathe and move into the moment. I promise this will keep you motivated, especially when you are about to do something that has nothing to do with your vision. It will be easier to tell yourself, I can wait until January to purchase those shoes with cash.

The awesome thing about having a vision is to know you will have many milestones along the way, as well as, obstacles, but keeping your mind focused on the prize will pay off in the long run. Celebrate your victories along the way. There will be nothing like experiencing that first bill paid off, especially if you have been making the minimum payment for years. And there will be nothing like the feeling you will get when you have completed your vision. Stick with it and don't be discouraged. Whatever you do, keep the vision before you always.

Now that you see yourself debt free, take it a step further by writing the vision and making it plain on the tablets, that he may run who reads it. "For the vision is yet for an appointed time; but at the end it will speak and it will not lie (Habakkuk 2:2-3, NKJV)."

ENDNOTES

1. Merriam-Webster's Medical Dictionary, © 2007. Retrieved from http://dictionary.reference.com/browse/vision.

EXERCISE – CHAPTER 4

1. **What financial road are you on right now? No more running. It's time to face your fears. Let the tears fall where they may, but today you are making a decision to change. Gather your financial records (checkbooks, bank statements for saving and checking accounts, credit reports with credit score, insurance policies and 401 k accounts). Write down where you are or what you need to improve.**

   _____
   _____
   _____

2. **Write a faith confession or motto you can use to encourage you on your financial journey. Example: I will owe no man nothing, but love or I can do all things through Christ who strengthens me.**

   _____
   _____
   _____

3. **Pray and ask the Lord where He would like you to co-labor with Him for financial freedom.**

   _____
   _____
   _____

PRAYER AND DECLARATION

Dear Father God, today I am making a choice to face my financially situation. I can't run from it any longer. I am on the wrong road, headed to the wrong destination. I got lost and did not ask for help because I was too embarrassed, self-willed, afraid, hurt and independent to ask for help. In fact I didn't want anyone to know I am lost, so I ignored my situation hoping that it would go away, made excuses because I didn't want to deal with it and blamed others because I didn't want to take responsibility for my own failures and disobedience. The road I am on is a disaster and I am ready to get off. Today, I take off the mask and repent for my actions and fears. Father, I am open to change. Please redirect my path and set me free from this bondage. Line upon line, precept upon precept, I will overcome and see the salvation of the Lord.

I decree and declare over my life, I can do all things through Christ who strengthens me. Therefore, I can and will live the abundant life Christ came to give me by being a good steward over my finances and taking responsibility for my actions. God's arm is not too short to save, so no matter how far I am out here financially today, God is able to bring me back to my rightful position. My ending will be greater than my beginning because today I am choosing to let go of my past and embrace my future. I can see it, so I can achieve it. All things are possible through Christ who strengthens me. AMEN

Chapter Five

WRITE THE VISION

Writing the vision and making it plain, means you are going to have to spend some time with your finances daily. You and your finances will become best friends, so make the best of it. Make it fun and exciting after all, this is your financial vision. The more detail you are in writing your financial vision, the more focused and discipline you will be. I choose to think, this exercise will also help you to become more responsible and savvy with your finances. You will begin to think about things you never thought about before. I promise you, the more you spend time with your finances, the more empowered you will feel because you know how much debt you are in, what you have to do to get out of it, and when you are going to get out.

The most amazing story I have to share is when my local church paid off a three million dollar ($3,000,000) mortgage in three years. I am sure when the Lord first placed this on my Pastor's heart, he thought it was impossible. I am sure others thought he was out of his mind too. One thing I know about my Pastor is when he gets a vision in his heart, nothing can stop him from fulfilling it. And I am sure he got the vision embedded in his mind, heart and spirit before he launched it to the house. I am even sure over the three years there were many bumps, hurdles and short comings, but nothing stopped my Pastor from keeping the vision before himself and the congregation. On Friday, March 31, 2006, the vision was fulfilled. The Antioch location was paid in full and we celebrated the victory.

I thank God and Bishop Walker for allowing me the opportunity to participate in something great. This experience changed my life in a way that is immeasurable. It changed my perception and thinking about my financial situation. I caught the vision for my own house. I began to see myself debt free. I said to myself, "If my church can pay a three million dollar debt in three years, then I can pay off my debt too. No longer will I settle for having student loan debt. No longer will I settle for paying a mortgage. No longer will I settle for having credit card debt. I have got to get back focused on my finances."

I asked the Lord to help me establish a vision for my finances. I had about fourteen thousand dollars ($14,000) in student loan debt and about six thousand dollars ($6,000) in credit card debt. I know it might have seemed logical to pay off the credit card debt first, but I chose to start with the student loan debt. I started with the student loan debt because two of the loans were in my mother's name and the other two loans were in mine. It was important to me to clear my mother of my debt but the balance in my name was less so I started there. It took me about two years to get it paid off, but it was worth the sacrifice.

The blessing is I did not tell my mother what I was doing. She was in shock when she received a letter telling her, my student loans were paid in full. And I was blessed because I watched God help me accomplish something that I did not think was possible. I also saw God do things with my finances that I had never seen before. When I made up my mind to do it, it was like God accelerated the process and turned water into wine. Even I do not know how I got those student loans paid off that fast, but God is truly faithful. As I am writing this book, I am working to pay off my credit card debt. According to my financial plan, my credit card debt should be paid in full by February 28, 2008. To be honest, it should have been paid off in June 2007, but again I got off track. I am telling you this so you will not get discouraged. And so you do not beat yourself up. Just repent for messing up and move forward. Don't stop until you see your vision completed.

My next goal is to get my savings account up to about ten thousand dollars ($10,000) or more by December 2008. Afterwards, I want to be the first one in my family to pay a mortgage off. Again I say, if my church can pay a mortgage off, then so can I. God is the same today, yesterday and forevermore (Hebrews 13:8). He is no respecter of persons, so what He does for one, He can do for another.

I'm telling you, creating a financial vision empowers you to see beyond where you are and into your financial future. It does not matter how long it takes you to get there, just get there. Take it day by day, step by step, and bill by bill. Get a motto to inspire you. My personal motto is "Owe no one anything except to love one another, for he who loves another has fulfilled the law (Romans 13:8, NKJV)." When I am feeling a little discouraged about not having a lot of money, my motto is "God shall supply all of my needs according to His riches in glory by Christ Jesus (Philippians 4:19, NKJV)."

Take the plunge! Do something you have never done before. See yourself beyond where you are, but see yourself through the eyes of Christ. He made you to be the head, not the tail, to be above, not beneath, a lender, and not a borrower (Deuteronomy 28:13). You are more than a conqueror in Christ Jesus who loves you (Romans 8:37). What is impossible for man is possible with God (Luke 18:27). Again, I remind you that you have to change your mindset, open your ears to listen, establish the vision, see the vision, and write the vision. Then work the vision because faith by itself, if not accompanied by action, is dead (James 2:17).

EXERCISE – CHAPTER 5

1. **Take a few minutes to dream financially? What you would like to accomplish financially with where you are right now, so I don't want you to dream about winning the lottery or someone coming along and paying all your bills off. This is about you putting in the hard work.**

   _____
   _____
   _____
   _____
   _____
   _____

PRAYER AND DECLARATION

Dear Father God, Your Word says, "Where there is no vision, the people will perish." I realize I have been walking without a vision for my life and finances; therefore, they are perishing. Father, give me the plan that You have for my life financially, make it plain to me and I will write it down so it will be always before me and others will help me run with it when it is read. Father, I surrender my control. I ask for Your good, perfect and acceptable will for my life and finances. I am tired of circling around in the wilderness, but I am ready to go to the promise land that is flowing with milk and honey. Father, I believe You will do exceedingly, abundantly, above and beyond all that I can ever even think or imagine.

I decree and declare over my life that I am a dream catcher. I not only see the vision, but I work the vision until I see it manifest. I am like Elijah the prophet; I am out running the chariots to a land that is flowing with milk and honey. I decree and declare over my life that I will never be broke another day of my life. Nothing is missing, lacking or broken in my life because I am a hearer and doer of the Word of God. His promises are yes and amen. I see, believe and receive my financial vision and destiny. AMEN

Chapter Six

MAKE IT PLAIN
❧

Now that you got your financial mental picture and you have started writing your financial vision, its time to make it plain. This is your opportunity to get as specific and detailed as possible. Here are a couple of suggestions to help you get started:

First, find out what your financial purpose is. Your financial purpose will be whatever you are striving for financially. It is why your finances exist. It is your aim or goal. The very thing you are pointing your finances to achieve, whether it is to be debt free, help others become debt free, start a business or give more, is your financial goal. Whatever that purpose is, write it down because you have to know why you are doing what you are doing financially. Initially, this may be very general, but keep brainstorming because this will help you to establish your Financial Statement of Purpose (FSoP).

Your FSoP will tell your personal story about your finances and why they exist. It will give you and your finances a clear road map to follow. You will know what your finances are designated to accomplish, who/what they are serving, why they are serving the person/thing, how long they will be serving and how the task will be accomplished. This statement will need to be as detailed as you can get. Remember, the sky is the limit. The more specific you are, the more focused you will be.

Secondly, think about your financial mission. A mission is a special assignment given to carry out a specific work. Your financial mission can be either short term or long term. This is your financial charge or order given. It will be through this thought process that you will be able to come up with your Financial Mission Statement (FMS).

Your FMS will contain some of the same things as your Financial Statement of Purpose; however, this statement will have more direction. It will be more focused. I like to call this your motivational statement, your financial motto because this will help others, like your family and friends, get excited about your financial vision. As you share this statement with others, they know where you are headed, why you are going in that direction and the end result. Before you know it, everyone will be singing your tune. Remember, you are not in this alone, the more people you have in agreement with you, the better you will be. It is these persons who will help you stay motivated, and cheer you on. The word of the Lord says, one can put one thousand to flight, but two can put ten thousand to flight (Deuteronomy 32:30). There is power in agreement.

Thirdly, establish Financial Values for yourself. Values are principles, standards or qualities considered worthwhile or desirable. In essence, what is the foundation of your finances? What is it standing on, you or God? There is an old cliché that says, "If you do not stand for something, you will fall for anything." With that in mind, I would establish my values based on the word of God because "His word does not return unto Him void, but it shall accomplish what He pleases, and it shall prosper in the thing for which He sent it (Isaiah 55:11, NKJV)." Your financial values are what you want God and others to say about your finances. Some ideal words would be faithful, integrity, character and consistency.

Finally, you want to establish Financial Goals. Goals are the purpose toward which an endeavor is directed. The Goal is the state of affairs that a plan is intended to achieve and when achieved, terminates behavior intended to achieve it. I know this phrase is a little confusing, but here is an example. You will work a part-time job for six months to pay off a credit card. Once the credit card is paid in full, you will stop working the part-time job. The only reason you were working the part-time job was to pay off the card. Now the purpose has been fulfilled, the part-time job is not necessary.

Your financial goals should line up with your financial vision, purpose, mission and values. They all must be on one accord. Your goals will tell you what you are setting out to accomplish, how you are going to accomplish the goal and the timeframe of the goal. These can be short term or long term. Please set as many short-term goals as possible, so you do not become overwhelmed.

Remember to celebrate yourself along the way, but use wisdom.

Before we move on to the next chapter, I would like to leave you with a little piece of wisdom I gained from reading an awesome book called Sister CEO by Cheryl D. Broussard. She states, "There are four A's of success: (1) attitude, (2) ambition, (3) assertiveness and (4) action."[1]

Up to now, I have been trying to get you to change your mindset, hearing, and vision, but now I want you to change your position. You have been doing things your way for a long time and it has gotten you where you are today. But it is time to release the control and hand it over to Jesus. Whether we believe it or not, He is the owner of everything, and we are just mere stewards, so take a walk with me back to the Garden of Eden. There are lessons to learn from the garden.

ENDNOTES

1. Cheryl D. Broussard, "Sister CEO: The Black Woman's Guide to Starting Your Own Business," New York: Penguin Group, 1997, p. 26.

EXERCISE – CHAPTER 6

** Please do not get overwhelmed with the below exercises or rush through them. Each one is very important to your financial future so don't rush through them. They might take you several days or weeks to accomplish.

1. A purpose is the reason something exists or why it is done. Write your Financial Statement of Purpose.

   _____
   _____
   _____
   _____

2. Values are principles, standards or qualities considered worthwhile or desirable. Write your financial values.

   _____
   _____
   _____
   _____

3. A vision is something that is or has been seen; the act or power of seeing or a vivid mental image. Write a Financial Vision Statement.

   _____
   _____
   _____
   _____

4. A mission is a special assignment given to carry out a specific work. Your financial mission can be either short term or long term. It

is your financial charge or order given. Write a Financial Mission Statement.

_____
_____
_____

5. Goals are the purpose toward which an endeavor is directed. Write your financial goals.

_____
_____
_____

6. A budget is a financial plan and roadmap. It puts a name and destination to every dollar that comes through your hands. Establish a budget for your finances.

_____
_____
_____

PRAYER AND DECLARATION

Dear Father God, I am getting a little overwhelmed by all of this and I need You to bring Your peace upon me. Show me the way and I will walk in it. Thank You for bringing Your wisdom and peace. You promised to keep me in perfect peace if I keep my mind stayed upon You. You promised to lead me to a path of righteousness if I would trust in You with all my heart and lean not to my own understanding, so Father, I am leaning on You to see me through.

Thank You for showing me my financial purpose, vision, mission, values, goals and budget. Thank you for my ending being better than my beginning. Thank You that I am on the right path and You are leading the way. I am excited about my present and future, so I leave my past behind. Thank You for the lessons learned and those to come. Thank You for Your faithfulness. Thank You for turning my mourning into dancing, my sorrow into joy, and my nights into days.

I decree and declare over my life, I am walking in the blessings and the favor of the Lord. Witty inventions and wealth are flowing to me. I am a visionary, a champion and an over-comer. I expect great things to manifest in my life spiritually, physically, mentally, emotionally, and financially. I am getting the Word rooted and grounded in my heart, mind and soul by meditating on it day and night. Therefore, I'm successful and growing by leaps and bounds. When I speak a word, it goes forth and accomplishes the very thing it was set out to accomplish and prospers in it regarding my life. I see my future and it is much brighter. AMEN

PART FOUR
Stewardship vs. Ownership

Chapter Seven

LESSONS FROM THE GARDEN

Matthew 25:14-15 - *"For the kingdom of heaven is like a man traveling to a far country, who called his own servants and delivered his goods to them (NKJV)."*

The first lesson I learned from this parable is God will go to any length to prosper you. In this parable, the man travels far into another country just to deliver his goods to his servants, whom he can trust. Now it is one thing for someone to have something for you and tell you to come get it. It is something very beautiful and special when that person is in another country and is willing to travel the distance to bring the gift they have for you to you. So let's not take this scripture lightly.

Biblical traveling was unlike today; they had to pretty much walk everywhere they went. Sometimes it took days, weeks or even months for them to get where they had to go. Wow, can you imagine someone loving you that much that they would travel for days, weeks or months just to bring you a gift they wanted you to have? Well I can and that someone's name is Jesus Christ. God believes in us so much He will search us out to bless us with His possessions, but not without preparing you for it first. He will never put more on us than we can bear. However, we must follow His instructions, so the blessing does not turn into a curse.

God shows us this through the story of Adam.

God made man into His own image and likeness. Therefore, Adam had everything he needed to fulfill God's command "to be fruitful and multiply; fill the earth and subdue it; and have dominion over the fish of the sea, over the birds of the air, and over every living thing that moves on the earth (Genesis 1:28, NKJV)." Then God placed Adam in the Garden of Eden, and gave him his first assignment. Adam was to tend and keep the garden with instructions not to eat from the tree of the knowledge of good and evil, or he would die (Read Genesis 2:15-17).

Adam was doing a great job, so he was promoted to naming the cattle, beast of the fields and the birds in the air. However, Adam did not know he was being prepared and set up for the ultimate blessing, naming his helpmate, the woman. Just think God already knew the assignment of tending and keeping up the garden, along with the animals would be a lot for Adam to do, so He was already working on making Adam a helper who was suitable for him before he even knew he would need one. Isn't it amazing how God is always ahead of us and has already answered our prayers before we even ask Him. Yet He allows us to go through a process and a series of events to prepare us to handle the next level blessing with character and integrity.

Can you imagine being given the assignment to name all the beast of the field and all the birds of the air that God formed out of the ground, in addition to tending and keeping the garden (Genesis 2:19)? What a great and awesome task. I wonder if Adam ever got overwhelmed and wanted to start complaining like many of us do in the midst of being processed for the blessing. I am going to be honest, my complaining would have sounded a little like this, first you want me to tend and keep this garden all by myself, and then you want me to name all of these animals? Jesus, please help a sister out.

However, Adam handled his task like a good steward and named all the animals and the birds that God presented to him. God was testing Adam to see what he would call each of the living creatures that He presented before him, but Adam did not name any of the living creatures his suitable helper (Genesis 2:20). So the Lord God caused Adam to fall into a deep sleep, and when he awoke, God presented her to Adam and he named her woman, for she was taken out of a man (Genesis 2:21-24). I wonder if Adam was communing with God in the process and listening for instructions on naming each of the living creatures that were brought before him. The reason I ask this question is because I wonder how Adam knew God had made the woman from the rib He had taken out of him? When I think about this question, the scripture that comes to mind is 1 Corinthians

2:16, which says, "For who has known the mind of the Lord that he may instruct him? But we have the mind of Christ (Read 1 Corinthians 2:1-16)." What a wonderful relationship Adam had with God, that he would know God's good, pleasing, and perfect will (Romans 12:2).

In order to be a good steward like Adam, we too must have an intimate relationship and consult Him in to know what His will is for our finances. One thing I am sure of is God will never give us more than we can bear, nor will He give us anything He has not prepared us for. But with each level of increase, there will come a greater testing and responsibility, so we have to stay focused more than ever due to the intensity of distractions, pressures and temptations that will come to get you off course. While on this journey to get debt free and stay debt free, we can't stop communing with God. We can't allow anyone's voice to become more powerful than God's in our lives. To bring this point to life, let's take another look at Adam.

In Genesis 2:16, the Lord told Adam he was free to eat from any tree in the garden; but the tree of the knowledge of good and evil, for when you eat of it you will surely die (NIV). Yet we find in Chapter 3 man had fallen. How did Adam get here because he knew better? Why did he allow Eve to talk him into eating from the tree of good and evil (Genesis 3:6-7)? Like Adam we have messed up. We have allowed everyone else's voice to become more powerful than God's in our finances. At this point, we have assumed the role of ownership, instead of stewardship. This leads to a road of destruction because we become prideful and most of all, we have stopped communing with God and listening to the Father's instructions in regards to our finances. There is a way that seems right to man, but in the end it leads to death (Proverbs 14:12).

Think how easy it is to get away from the Lord, paying tithes and offering were easy when we were making a hundred dollars, but now we are making five figures or even six figures; ten percent has become too much to give. We were sold out for Christ when we didn't have a date or a mate, but now the things of God take a back seat. The choices that Adam and Eve made in the garden still affect us today, and our decisions will affect future generations. When we choose to be disobedient to God, we suffer consequences for our sins. The wages of sin is death (Romans 6:23), whether spiritually, physically, emotionally, mentally or financially. But there is hope, a way out it's called repentance, which means asking the Lord for forgiveness and turning away from the sin that so easily ensnare us, fulfilling the lusts of the flesh and doing things our own way. Take the challenge today, make the decision to invite God back into your finances and assume your rightful position as a steward. So what does it mean to be a steward versus an owner? According to the American Heritage College Dictionary, a steward is one who manages another's property, finances, or other affairs.[1]

To be a steward you must realize you are only a manager of your finances, just as Adam was only a manager of the Garden of Eden. God has placed a certain amount of income into our hands. He fully trusts that we will do the right thing and follow His principles and instructions. As we are obedient and responsible, then God will promote us. When we are faithful over a few things, God will make us rulers over much (Matthew 25:23). Psalm 75:6-7, reminds us, "No one from the east or the west or the desert can exalt a man. But it is God who judges: He brings one down, and he exalts another (NIV)."

An owner is someone who possesses and is independent of outside help or control. So if we consider ourselves to be the owner of our finances then we are totally responsible for the well being of them outside the help of God. We bear the burden and assume the position as provider. Therefore, it will be up to us to figure out how to get ourselves out of the financial trouble we are in. Do not take this position in your own life, it will be like the curse of Adam on your life (Genesis 3:17-19).

You will find yourself working a second job and getting nowhere with everyone in the house tired to the bone and frustrated. And after all of that working, you will still find yourself in the same situation or worse because you have now trained yourself to live off of a temporary income that became permanent. I am not against working a second job, but only if God told you to do it. Trying to do it on your own can even lead you to do other ungodly things you never thought you would do. Debt is bondage and people will do just about anything to get out of it. However, I am going to assume you will do like I did and get a second job, so here is my testimony.

There was a time in my life when God gave me the strength and ability to work a second job to get out of debt. I knew it was Him because I went into this retail store and got hired on the spot. I knew what I wanted to bring home each week to meet my financial goal. I told the manager what I wanted to make, and she gave it to me without question. In fact, I made more than the other employees and I was working part-time. I realize it was favor on my life, and God was honoring my obedience to get my finances in order. He was also teaching me a lesson about pride and being dependent on Him, instead of self and my degree.

You see, I thought because I had a degree that I shouldn't have to work a second job. Oh, but God cleared that up fast. It got so bad, I had to get a second job, but He blessed me when I surrendered. And now I realize God was only preparing me for my future. I went through that experience for this book. It was only God that gave me a plan to use my part-time income to get out of debt, and to live off my full time income. I think I worked part-time for about a year. I got several debts paid down. In addition, I was able to get an apartment without a roommate and everything I needed was paid in full. Then that job dried up. God wanted me to know He would take care of me without a second job. I didn't think I could make it living alone, but God showed me otherwise.

About two years later, God allowed me to work another part-time job. Again, I knew it was God because I had been praying for a part-time job doing bookkeeping. I didn't want to do another retail job. Again, I got hired on the spot, making about the same as I did in retail, but for less hours a week. Plus I was doing something I loved to do. I worked this job for about a year. Again I got some other debts paid off and established a savings account. Once again, God blessed me for my obedience. This time I was blessed with buying my first home. And again, God dried up the second job.

Things got tight again, so I did what I knew to do, I got a second job. Like the gentleman God is, He let me go right ahead. I found the perfect part-time job, grading papers for about ten dollars an hour. I thought this was easy money. I was able to pay off some more debt. I know you are like, how much debt was she in? As I stated in the first chapter, you have to change your mindset, and start listening. I would get out of debt and get right back in it. I was not fully relying upon God. Anyway, I made it through my first assignment with this job. You would work about a month or two, and then they would call you back when they received another grading assignment. Well, I got a call back, but this time it was different. The blessing became a curse for me.

I was worn out, frustrated, angry and mad. I couldn't figure it out because it was easy work. I started complaining. Yes I was getting debt paid down, but my attitude was suffering. I was like, "Lord, I will be glad when this assignment is up." I heard the Lord say to me, "Stop complaining because you never asked me if you could work a second job. You did this one on your own. You do not trust me to get you out of debt. You do not believe I will take care of you. And you will not quit this assignment, until it is over. The next time, you will ask me if working a part-time job is My will for your life." And you know, I haven't worked a part-time job since and God has been faithful to take care of me. The lesson I learned is what

God allows in one season of your life, He doesn't allow in the next season. He takes us from glory to glory. We have to always be willing to listen to Him and follow Him.

Bottom line, before you go out and do the worldly things; make sure you are first doing the heavenly things to reach financial freedom. The first and foremost thing is to repent for being irresponsible with the finances God has released into your hands. If you confess your sins, He is faithful and just to forgive you of all your sins and cleanse you from all unrighteousness (1 John 1:9, NKJV). There is no condemnation in Christ Jesus (Romans 8:1, NKJV). The moment you repent and ask for forgiveness, it is done, erased and finished. But I dare not tell you, you will not suffer consequences for the sin, just like I did in trying to do things my own way. However, I am a better and stronger person for it, plus I have the privilege just like you to help someone else not to do what I have done. Remember, all things work together for the good of those who love the Lord and are called according to His purpose (Romans 8:28, NKJV).

Secondly, seek first the kingdom of heaven and all His righteousness, then all these things will be added unto you (Matthew 6:33, NKJV). This means to seek out God's principles, statutes, commandments and laws. These are the things God will use to give you tools, strategies, and tactics to obtain financial freedom. I can't promise that you will come out of your financial situation overnight, but I promise that you will come out right. God is not a hocus pocus God. He is not into magic, but He is into miracles. He performs miracles as He pleases, whether it is giving you the grace to work a second job, having someone sow a seed into your life, giving you an increase on your job, or just plain supernaturally eliminating your debt. The key is not to put God in a box or put restraints on Him. Follow His principles of paying your tithes, offerings and first fruit. Trust me, His principles work, I have seen them show up in every area of my life.

Thirdly, surrender your financial situation to the Lord. He sees far ahead of you. He already knows, the date, hour, minute, and second your financial situation will end. When you surrender, you release all control over to Christ Jesus. Give Him free reign to do as He pleases, the way He pleases. Make a decision to trust and rely on Him. Please do not do what I did. Don't give it to God and then take it back. He is a gentleman, and will never force Himself on you. He will let you run it if you want to run it. Eventually, you come to the end of yourself. Do your part as the steward and He will do His part as the Owner. Most of all don't ignore the Owner's voice when He is speaking, He will save you from a lot of trouble and also from yourself.

Remember when you were a child doing something your mother told you not to do, but you decided to do your own thing, and while you were doing it, you would hear her voice saying, "Don't do that." The next thing you knew, you were busted or the very thing she said would happen, happens. You find yourself saying, "Mama told me not to do it. I should have listened."

God is the same way. He is always talking to us, telling us what to do and not to do with our finances. Just like mother, He tells you because He wants the best for you. He knows the outcome. However, are we listening to the still small voice when He tells us no, wait, and even yes? I think we miss the still small voice of God because we want God to yell at us or perform some sign, miracle or wonder to stop us. He has given us the Holy Spirit within us to lead, guide and direct us into all truths, but it is up to us to be sensitive to the Spirit (John 16:13). Pay attention to how unsettling you are feeling. Take a few minutes to find out what it is all about. Is it fear or is it God stretching you?

A wise woman once said to me, "You can have God's permissive will, or you can have His perfect will. When you receive His perfect will, you will always receive what was truly meant for you and no one can take it away from you, but God, Himself. His perfect will always happens in His timing, not yours. His permissive will gives you what you want when you want it so you can find out you were not ready for what you thought you wanted."

Don't settle for God's permissive will in your finances, but accept His perfect will. Be willing to change. Do not continue to do the things you have been doing that have caused you to be unsuccessful with your finances. Go to the Father and ask Him what He wants you to do with what He has searched you out to deliver into your hands. He promised, "If you bring your tithes and offering into the storehouse He will open up the windows of heaven and pour you out a blessing that you will not have room enough to receive and you can test Him at His word (Malachi 3:10, NKJV).

Learn the lessons from the garden. All God is asking you to do with the finances is to maintain and keep the garden, which is His kingdom. And He will be the burden bearer and the provision maker. He will be the one who gives you seed to sow into the kingdom. He is the one who has given you the power to get wealth, and that wealth is not just for you (Deuteronomy 8:18, NKJV).

I know this was a tough Chapter, so go through the emotions. God will heal. Take a few minutes to breathe. Meditate on the goodness of Christ Jesus. Be encouraged because God is not finished with you yet. He is faithful to complete the good work He has begun in you (Philippians 1:6, NKJV). You are not alone in this race. Remember, we are doing this together. Plus He promised to never leave you nor forsake you (Hebrews 13:5, NKJV). It is not by your might, nor by your power, but by the Spirit of the Lord that you shall come out as pure gold (Zechariah 4:6, NKJV).

ENDNOTES

1. The American Heritage Dictionary, Third Edition, Houghton Mifflin Company, Boston: MA, pp.1333 & 977.

EXERCISE – CHAPTER 7

At this point, I want you to read Genesis Chapter 2, as well as, Matthew 25. I believe God has a specific revelation for you. Take a look at where you are financially. Ask yourself some hard questions based on what you have read in this section. Write those things down, along with the solutions God place upon your heart.

_____
_____
_____
_____
_____
_____
_____
_____

PRAYER AND DECLARATION

Dear Father God, thank You for loving me so much. Thank you for the gifts that you have given me and are giving me. You said in your word, "Every good and perfect gift comes from above and it adds no sorrow." You promised me that You would never leave me nor forsake me so I am not on this journey alone and I can trust that You will lead and guide me by Your Holy Spirit. I recognize that all things are possible through You who lives within me; therefore, I can conquer debt and everything else that will try to hold me captive in my life. I am the righteousness of Christ and I am victorious, no matter what things look like. You hold the keys to the kingdom and I can call those things which are not as though they were because You have given me the power to bring heaven down to earth.

Father I release all control and I submit myself, will, and emotions to you because You are the Potter and I am the clay. You are the Owner and I am the steward. The earth is Yours and the fullness thereof. And what You have for me is for me. So nothing is missing, lacking or broken in my life. I can trust you to provide all that I need as I co-labor with You by being obedient and submissive to Your will, way and purpose for my life. Thank You, Father for making all things new in my life.

Chapter Eight

DOUBLE OR NOTHING

Matthew 25:15 - *"And to one he gave five talents, to another two, and to another one, to each according to his own ability; and immediately he went on a journey (NKJV)."*

As stated in my last chapter, God is a God of process. He will allow you to experience situations and circumstances tailor made to develop you for the next level blessing. When we are faithful over the few things, then He makes us rulers over much more (Matthew 25:23, NKJV). This is why we can kick, holler and scream for something in our twenties, but not receive it until we are thirty. God gives us blessings according to our ability to handle them. He does this because He does not want you to be overwhelmed, disgusted or discouraged. Plus He does not want you to mishandle the blessing when you get it. God does not operate in failure. He will not give you anything to set you up for failure, but to set you up for a blessing. He has equipped you with everything you need to complete the assignment. This is why God has allowed you to be blessed the way you are blessed. You can handle what He has given you.

When we look at Matthew 25:15, we see after the man left, the one with the five talents knew exactly what to do with the talents he had been given. He immediately went to do some trading and gained five more talents. This servant followed the principles God gave us in Genesis 1:28, to be fruitful and multiply. God has placed within us both natural and spiritual gifts to complete the calling and assignments placed upon our lives. I choose to believe this servant even used some of his natural talents to double his money. He had to know a little about negotiating and investing in order to know when to put his money into the system and when to take it out to get the best return.

Likewise, the servant who received the two talents went out and doubled the money placed in his hands also. Now the story does not tell what he did in order to double the two talents, but we can safely assume he put the money to work to give him the best return. The amazing thing about the servant with the two talents is he did not complain about receiving two talents. He just focused on what he had in his hand and how to multiply it. He had a plan and the plan was to double what he had received.

Too many times, we get discouraged because we are comparing ourselves with someone else. But God has blessed us right where we are. You cannot handle where they are and they cannot handle where you are either. For example, we hear about wealthy people loosing their mind, committing suicide or go on killing rampages just because they lost everything or had to downgrade in lifestyle. But here you are being strong and content in the Lord, until your promotion comes. They can't handle where you are. And think about those who win the lottery. Many of them are worse off than they were before they won the money. Some of them even loose their mind and commit suicide because of all the pressures that comes with being wealthy. Others end back up broke, busted and disgusted because they did not change their mindset nor listen to the Holy Spirit's wisdom concerning their finances.

The lesson in this story is no matter what God places in your hands, He has given you the power to get wealth (Deuteronomy 8:18, NKJV), so you are able to double what you have. It is up to you to work it and be faithful with it and the increase will come. God is no respecter of persons; what He does for one, He will do for another. He gave both of the servants the ability to double their money and no matter how much they had, they both reaped the same reward by following the principles of God and doing what they knew how to do.

Now, let's consider the servant who received one talent. Instead of doing what he could do with the talents he received, he allowed his emotions, feelings and attitude to get in the way of the blessing. Therefore, he chose to dig a hole in the ground and hide the master's money. The problem with this servant is he had a negative attitude towards his master. He was concerned that his master would take the increase from him. In other words, he thought his master was a harsh man and a robber. He told his master that he knew he would reap where he had not sown and gather where he had not scattered seed.

Too many times, this same mentality takes place in the body of Christ when it comes to giving. We get too caught up in what we think someone will do with the money so we miss our blessing. Your first priority in giving should be pleasing God, and edifying and building His kingdom. If God has told you to give something, and the leaders do something crazy with the money, they will be accountable to God. He will handle them. You just do what He has commanded you to do.

Another thing, we cannot allow the status of another person to determine how much we will give. We don't pay our tithes and offering because we look at the leader who might be blessed and say, "I am not paying my tithes to a man. He's already got enough. He is not struggling for anything, but I am. So he is not going to miss my little funds so I will just keep mine." I must say, this is a wrong attitude. We do not pay our tithes unto a man; we give them to God. It is God's command that we do so and He is the one who blessed you with it anyway.

It amazes me how people do not want to invest into the kingdom of God, but when it comes to sowing into the things of the world, we have no problem. We do not mind paying one hundred dollars or more to go see a celebrity perform, even though they are a millionaire. The problem is they have not done one thing for you. They have not poured one positive thing into you the whole time you have been in their presence, but when it comes to the men and women of God, we have a problem, whether they are wealthy or not. Therefore, we miss the blessing God wanted to pour out on our lives. And it blows my mind, how we think the people of God are not supposed to have anything. But it is okay for NBA players, football players, entertainers, and actors to live in mansions and have ten cars they can't drive? Oh the devil is a liar, but that is another story.

To be honest, if this is your attitude, I would like to challenge you to re-evaluate where you are and why you are there. I would not be a part of something that I do not want to invest in. If you feel this way about the church you are attending, the job you are working at, relationship you are in or the possessions that you have, then please consider releasing them because you might find out you are holding onto something you should be releasing or you have put yourself in a comfortable place and it is time to move forward because your heart is not there. Please do not take this the wrong way or justification to walk away from things you have not put an effort into. It is just human nature to invest and put our best into the things we want. Surely you would not move into a house and not take care of it. If you don't, it is going to fall apart. This is just a revelation God is giving us in the midst of the lesson; perhaps He is challenging you to think differently or to let something go.

The question I had about this story is how did the other two servants know what the master wanted and the third servant didn't? I wonder what type of relationship each of the servants had with their master or did the other two servants choose to honor their master regardless of what they thought about him? Your relationship with Jesus Christ is very important. It is through private intimate time with the Lord that you will come to know His character, nature, values, likes, dislikes and expectations. Romans 12:1-2 tells us our reasonable service is to present our bodies as a living sacrifice, holy, and pleasing to God, and not to conform to this world, but be transformed by the renewing of our minds that you may prove what is that good, pleasing and perfect will of God for your life (NIV). The Lord wants you to try Him at his word and see that He will not throw open the floodgates of heaven and pour so much blessing that you will not have room enough for it (Malachi 3:10). Trust Him to be the Master over your finances, and be responsible with what He has given unto you. Don't be afraid to use the gifts and talents He has given you along with Godly wisdom, knowledge and understanding to multiply the money He has placed in your hand. He promised, those who are faithful over a few things will be rulers over much (Matthew 25:23, NKJV).

EXERCISE – CHAPTER 8

** Read 2 Kings 4:1-7. As you read this passage of scripture think about yourself and what God has given you that can set you free from financial bondage.

1. List some of your spiritual gifts, talents and skills. **Spiritual gifts** are spiritual abilities endowed upon you by the Holy Spirit (gift of wisdom, discernment, prophecy, and healing). **Talents** are genetically given abilities that just come natural (singing, mathematics, and art). **Skills** are abilities you have acquired through study or someone else (Accountant, Engineer, and Electrician)

_____
_____
_____
_____

2. What has the Lord put on your heart to do with the gifts, talents, and skills He has put in your hands?

_____
_____
_____

3. Think about the 3 servants we read about above, which one are you? Think about why you are not using the gifts, talents and skills God has placed in your hands? Is it fear, procrastination or wisdom, knowledge, or understanding?

Kingdom Finances for Kingdom Building

_____
_____
_____

4. What part do these gifts, talents and skills play in your financial freedom? How can you use them to be a service and blessing to others?

_____
_____
_____

PRAYER AND DECLARATION

Dear Father God, You said if anyone lacks wisdom, he could ask and you would give it to him. Father, I am asking you for the wisdom, knowledge and understanding regarding the gifts, talents and skills you have placed within. Why have You given them to me and how would You like me to use them to be a blessing to others in this world? How do these gifts, talents and skills play a part in my financial freedom? Father, You said, we have not because we ask not, so I am bringing this matter before Your throne to reason it all out with You. You have the master plan for my life, so I surrender and submit to Your will, way and plan for my life.

Father, reveal to me those wrong mindsets and attitudes that I have that are hindering me from being fruitful and multiplying that which you have placed in my hands. What am I holding onto that is dead in my life or not of You? Father, I ask You to break the spirit of poverty off of my life and the hold that it has on my mindset.

I decree and declare over my life that I am a servant of the Most High God. I have the mind of Christ and I will not fear the unknown. God, You did not give me the spirit of fear and because of that I have power, love and a sound mind. I am great in Your eyes and I will not be afraid or dismayed. I can slay Goliath like David, march into the promise land like Joshua, and like Moses, I will meet with You face to face to receive Your instructions and revelations. I can conquer all of mine enemies and possess the promise land that you have given me to partake. I am like a well-watered garden and a spring whose waters never fail. Everything connected to me will grow and prosper. I can release and let go of things. I do not have to hoard or be greedy because there is more than enough to go around. And I believe as I release, God, You will bring the increase. AMEN!!!

PART FIVE

GIVING

Chapter Nine

TWO FISH AND FIVE LOAVES

John 6:8 - *"Here is a boy with five small barley loaves and two small fish, but how far will they go among so many (NIV)?"*

Typically when we read the testimony about Jesus feeding the five thousand, we normally focus on the miracle Jesus performed. However; there is a financial blessing within this passage of scripture. In this parable, there are five thousand men, besides the women and children that need to be feed for the Passover Feast. The disciples are wondering will they ever be able to meet a need so great. Jesus tests the disciples by asking them, "Where shall we buy bread for these people to eat?" Philip, one of the disciples, answers, "Eight months wages would not buy enough bread for each one to have a bite." Then another disciple, Andrew, Simon Peter's brother, spoke up, "Here is a boy with five small barley loaves and two small fish, but how far will they go among so many (Read John 6:1-15)?"

This dialogue as a whole blesses me because Jesus' original question was never about what was needed or how the need was going to be met. It was about where to go to get the need met, or who could supply what was needed? Yet, the disciples told Jesus the problems of fulfilling the need. Philip never saw the miracle. He like most of us couldn't see the forest for the trees, so he told Jesus they didn't have enough time or money to meet the need, so why bother. And Andrew, at least found a solution to the need, but minimized the value of what he found and what it was capable of doing, when put into the right hands.

How many times do we do exactly what the disciples did when God places us in a position to meet a need? How many times, do we do this with the finances Jesus puts into our hand to meet a need? If all we have to give to a person or vision is two pennies, we miss the blessing of giving the gift because we minimize the value of what we have in our hands. Therefore, we make the decision not to give at all. When it comes to the provisions of Jesus Christ, it is all about our perception and what we see. We must look with our spiritual eyes, not our natural eyes or we will find the environment around us great.

This reminds me of the spies that Moses sent into the promise land. Only Caleb and Joshua came back with a good report and the belief they could possess the land. The other spies said, the giants in the land were too great, and they minimized themselves as grasshoppers. Well, you can guess who got the reward. If you guessed Caleb and Joshua, you are right (Read Numbers 13). In the Master's hands little becomes much. He promised that He would do exceedingly, abundantly, above and beyond what we can ever think or imagine with the power within us (Romans 3:20, NKJV). That power comes from the Holy Spirit. I know I took another side bar. Let's get back to the scripture at hand.

The blessing in the text was everything small, yet valuable to the fulfillment of the need. The person who had what they needed was small; a child instead of an adult and the amount of food needed was a small amount. Maybe the bread and the fish were not small, but that is the way Andrew perceived it since the need was so great. So when he found the young boy with the two fish and five loaves of barley, he looked at the people and looked at the fish and bread and said, "It was small." I wonder what Andrew would have said if it was just the twelve disciples, Jesus and the young boy. I am going to let you ponder on that for a minute. Instead of looking at this scenario from the perspective of the disciples, place your name with theirs and see where your faith is with the Source.

Now that we have seen this text from the perspective of the disciples, let's look at it from the perspective of the young boy who had exactly what they needed. It must have been exciting for the young boy to have what the masses needed. However, the first thing I see with the young boy is he came with the intent to meet a need. He was prepared, but he had to make a sacrifice. How many times do we keep what we have in our hand because we only have a little, so we feel reluctant to share or give? This is a spirit of poverty and selfishness. The spirit of poverty says there is not enough so I will hoard because I have to take care of my needs before I can ever meet anyone else. It believes my needs will not get met, so I have to keep all I got or I have to do someone else wrong in order to get my needs met. Ask yourself, why was the boy, the only one who brought something with him and the others did not? Now with that in mind, who are you most like, the boy, the masses or the disciples? The reason I add the masses is because they did not bring anything.

EXERCISE – CHAPTER 9

1. In regards to your financial situation, who do you think most like, Philip, Andrew or the little boy? What has framed this pattern of thinking in your life?

   _____
   _____
   _____
   _____

2. What area of giving do you need to invite and trust God in? Is it in the area of giving, tithing, sowing or all three? What is hindering you from trusting the Lord?

   _____
   _____
   _____
   _____

3. Do you believe in the vision that your Pastor has set for the house and if you do not belong to a local church, I challenge you to think of a ministry that you do believe in their vision and sow into it on a constant and regular basis?

   _____
   _____
   _____
   _____

PRAYER AND DECLARATION

Dear Father God, help me to see past my financial situation and become the giver that You have destined for me to be. Your Word says, "Give and it shall be given unto me pressed down, shaken together and running over." You said the one thing I can test You in is the area of tithing and You will open up the windows of heaven and pour me out a blessing that I do not have room enough to receive, but I must not rob from you any more in the area of tithes and offering.

Father, lay a burden upon me in the area of giving so I do my part to advance the kingdom of heaven here on this earth. Give me a holy passion and a thirst to want to help others, despite what I see in my bank account. God I trust you will give me wisdom to know what soil to sow seed into. And I promise I will not entertain the spirit of poverty that tries to keep me in bondage from giving in freedom and liberty. Father, I invite You into the area of giving for my life and I surrender to Your will and way. I will give where, when and the amount You tell me to give without questioning or analyzing why. And as I release, I know You will replenish because You are the One who gives seed to the sower.

I decree and declare over my life that my mind has been renewed and transformed. I see the vision of Jesus Christ and it is to spread the gospel throughout the world. I will no longer think small, but I will possess a spirit of Caleb and Joshua and know that there is nothing that I cannot overcome. I am victorious over the spirit of poverty and it will no longer control what I sow into the kingdom. I will be radical for Christ, as well as, obedient. Father, You said for me to bring the whole tithe into the storehouse, as well as, the offering and I will do so diligently and consistently. As I release, other lives will be forever impacted. This is my reasonable service to You. I will not worry about what tomorrow will hold for it will take care of itself. Father if you take care of the birds of the air and lilies of the field, then I know You will provide for me. I will trust You with my whole heart and I will not lean to my own understanding for You own the world and the fullness thereof and I am the righteousness of Christ and an heir to Your throne. AMEN

Chapter Ten

DON'T BLOCK YOUR BLESSINGS

Malachi 3:10 - *"Bring the whole tithe into the storehouse, that there may be food in My house. Test Me in this, says the LORD Almighty (NIV)"*

Let's take a look at Malachi 3:8-12, which talks about tithing. The reason we give the tithe is so there will be food in the house of the Lord. This food will take care of, nourish and feed the people. Typically, this is done through ministry work of all kind. The food also takes care of those who work full time for the church. If you don't believe me, then go to Deuteronomy 14, it talks about the tithing principle and why the tithe exists.

First and foremost, the tithe is given so you will always fear the Lord your God (Deuteronomy 14:23, NKJV). Fearing the Lord is about reverencing, honoring and respecting the Lord. It is about relationship with Him, not being afraid.

Think about it. Would you want to be in a relationship where the person does not ever put you first, but the focus is always about them. They are not willing to invest in you or the things you believe in? I can answer this one for you, "No." Then why do we do God this way?

Typically when we want to know someone in the natural, we immediately invest our money into them by taking them out on dates, driving to see them or even buying gifts. Well, it works the same in the spiritual realm. God's word even tells us if you want to know where a man's heart is, look and see where he puts his treasures (Matthew 6:21). His treasure is his money. I promise if I go through your checkbook or better yet your checking account, I will find out where most of your money is going. The sad thing about it is the places where you are investing most of your money are not reaping you a harvest, or a return. However, God promises us a return when we invest in His kingdom and the people who serve His kingdom. Yes, I got you right there. Yes, we must also invest in those who serve God's kingdom.

Deuteronomy 14:27 states, "You shall not forsake the Levite who is within your gates, for he has no part nor inheritance with you (NKJV)." The reason why the Lord said this is because He would be the One who is their share and their inheritance (Numbers 18:20). Another reason we take care of the men and women of God is because their responsibility is to the house of God. Just like the Levites, they are responsible for bearing the offenses against the sanctuary and to take care of it. The Lord tells us, "He will bless us in all the work of our hands that we do when we take care of His servants and people (Deuteronomy 14:29, NKJV)."

Last but definitely not least, God wants to bless us as stated above. He said, "We can test Him at tithing, and see if He will not open up a window of heaven and pour us out blessings that we have not room enough to receive (Malachi 3:10, NKJV)." He will bless all the work of our hands. He will rebuke the devourer for our sakes. God is trying to simultaneously get a blessing to us, as well as, a blessing through us. Plus when we are obedient to His Word, He always promises to bless us (Read Deuteronomy 28). One thing I want to make clear to you is we do not do anything for the Lord to reap His blessings. Anything we do for Him should be because we love Him and are in a covenant relationship with Him. If we love Him, we will obey Him (John 14:15). Again I remind you the first reason He gave us for tithing is so we will fear Him (Deuteronomy 14:23, NKJV).

EXERCISE – CHAPTER 10

1. What attitude have you developed against your leader that hinders you from being obedient to God's Word to bring all the tithes and offering into the storehouse?

   _____
   _____
   _____
   _____

2. Take inventory of your checkbook/checking account. Is God at the center of your finances, if not what are you afraid of?

   _____
   _____
   _____
   _____

3. Think of a time when you honored God in giving to the kingdom. What happened as a result of your giving?

   _____
   _____
   _____
   _____

PRAYER AND DECLARATION

Dear Father God, help me to transform my mind in the area of giving because I want to reference You in all that I do, as well as, with the finances You have called me to steward. Father, I do not want to fix my eyes upon man, but I want to trust the God within me to give with freedom and liberty. I don't want to give and worry about what I have invested in the kingdom. You promised that I have the Holy Spirit within to lead, guide and direct me into all truth, so I ask You to always lead, guide and direct me into truth when giving and sowing into the kingdom. Father, I trust that You will never let me be deceived or carried away by my own desires when it comes to investing in the kingdom. Your Word is free; therefore, I do not have to buy a healing, prophecy, word of knowledge, word of wisdom, deliverance or anything that You promised me I can have in your Word. I will listen to the Holy Spirit and the spirit of discernment that You have placed on the inside of me.

Because You are a Father that would not have me be deceived, I trust You, Father, to plant me with a leader who has financial character, integrity, and accountability. Therefore, I can give liberty to the vision that has been set before the house. I can also sow liberally into other ministries that You place on my heart to give, knowing I am advancing Your kingdom throughout this earth to those who need to hear and see You the most.

I decree and declare over my life that I do not have the spirit of fear, but power, love and a sound mind. I do not have a poverty mentality, but a prosperous mentality. I am like a revolving door, as I give out, it comes back to me in order for me to give out of myself again. Nothing in my life is missing, lacking or broken. I am a well-watered garden whose leaves will never wither away. God is my Source and Resource so I do not have to be afraid to sow into His kingdom.

I decree and declare over my life and finances that God is Lord, which means He is the Authority and Ruler over them so I know I do not have to worry or doubt where He leads me to plant, for His plans are never to harm me, but to prosper me and to give me a hope and a future.

I decree and declare that I am one who will support and carry the leader that I have been given to feed me the Word, trusting not in them, but the Lord that has lead me under their authority. I am an investor and a beneficiary of the vision of my leader; therefore, I will do my part to ensure that I carry the load and the burden also. AMEN.

Chapter Eleven

YOU REAP WHAT YOU SOW

❧

Haggai 1:5-6 *- "Give careful thought to your ways. You have planted much, but have harvested little. You eat, but never have enough. You drink, but never have your fill. You put on clothes, but are not warm. You earn wages, only to put them in a purse with holes in it (NIV)."*

One of the most miraculous times of worship in the church has become one of the most depressing times in the church, offering time. Why? We are in financial bondage. It amazes me even in my own personal life that we determine what we will put in church based on the bills we have, or we won't give because we are focused on who will get the money. However, when it comes to worldly things, we do not think twice about what we will give, despite our financial situation. Before you buy that CD you want for fifteen dollars, do you say to yourself, "I have bills that need to be paid?" Do you even think about the financial situation of the artist and what they will do with the money you just sowed into their life? Again, I ask, why do we do this when it comes to the things of God and the leaders who labor in the field for the kingdom?

When we want something in the world, we will find a way to get it, even if it means paying a bill late, borrowing money from friends/relatives, or charging it.

But when that one opportunity comes to sow into the kingdom of God, which is sure to reap a harvest and return, we become cheap or even critical, and some of us give with an attitude. Then we wonder why we are in financial bondage, or why the Lord doesn't answer our prayers concerning financial increase.

Let's face it; we have not been faithful over the little things so God cannot make us rulers over much. We have not followed God's principles in giving. And most of all, our hearts have not been right. But God is so gracious and merciful to forgive us. So we as a people must repent, and ask Him to forgive us. Remember, He is faithful and just to forgive us of all our sin and cleanse us from all unrighteousness (1 John 1:9, NKJV).

I just want you to take a couple of minutes to think about this. What if someone gave you a gift, but there was conditions with the gift? You have to buy what they want you to buy, where they tell you to buy it or you can forget it. You wouldn't want the gift, now would you? What if someone presented you with a gift, but you could tell they didn't want to give you the gift? Would you want the gift? What if someone you loved gave you a gift that was clearly leftovers of what they had, would you want that gift? I am sure; your answer to all of these questions is "No." However, every time we have an opportunity to sow into the kingdom, we display this attitude without conviction or conscience. So I challenge you, the next time you have an opportunity to sow into His kingdom, ask Him what He would like for you to give, check your heart and make sure you are giving Him the best. I promise you will feel Him smiling, just like you smile when you receive heartfelt gifts.

EXERCISE – CHAPTER 11

1. Read Haggai 1:5-11. Does this sound like your finances? The more you make the more you need and the less you seem to have. If so find out why by asking the Lord what you are doing wrong? You might already know. Find the truth in the Word.

   _____
   _____
   _____
   _____

2. Last chapter, I asked you to take inventory of your checkbook/checking account, but this chapter, I am asking you to take inventory of your heart and attitude towards giving. Do you have a giving heart and attitude?

   _____
   _____
   _____
   _____

3. Are you sowing more into the world than the kingdom? What benefits are you gaining from doing so? What is it costing you?

   _____
   _____
   _____
   _____

PRAYER AND DECLARATION

Dear Father God I am coming before You to reason out my finances. I realize that I have not been honoring You the way that I should. I have been sowing more into the things of the world than Your kingdom. I have allowed something that I am supposed to have control over to control me; therefore, I am in financial bondage. I realize financial bondage is more than being in debt, but it is also a mindset, which affects my behavior, values and perspective. I can be free from debt, yet in financial bondage mentally. I should be able to give cheerfully with joy.

I have been just like those in Haggai 1:1-11, and I repent of my sins and I ask for Your forgiveness. Father I need Your help if I am going to be free from financial bondage. Father, reveal my heart, thoughts and behaviors to me. I want to get to the root of the problem and return unto You. Father, take control of my finances and I promise I will follow You. I surrender my will for Yours. Thank You for giving me another opportunity to get it right.

I decree and declare the past is left behind and I am beholding the new things God has planned for my life. Father, I am a giver and I am multiplying Your kingdom. You are the ultimate Financial Advisor, so I will consult You in every financial transaction no matter how big or small. Father, thank You for giving me a new heart and a right spirit. Thank You for transforming my mind, thoughts and behaviors. I decree and declare as for me and my house; we will serve You with all the days of our lives. AMEN.

PART SIX

CHECKBOOK MANAGEMENT

Chapter Twelve

SETTING ORDER IN YOUR FINANCES

1 Corinthians 14:26-40 -*"Let all things be done decently and in order (NKJV)."*

Everything in life has a DNA structure, which is the blueprint of life. It is life's instruction manual. According to DNA Forensics, an article published by Human Genome Projection Information website, "DNA can provide insights into many intimate aspects of a person and their families including susceptibility to particular diseases, legitimacy of birth and perhaps predispositions to certain behaviors."[1]

Just as DNA is the blueprint of life, your checkbook register is the blueprint of your financial transactions. However, the information is only as good as the information recorded. Assuming you keep good records, your checkbook register will tell where the treasures of your heart lie. It can also tell someone whether you are detailed oriented or not, and what your strengths and weaknesses are. I like to say, "Your checkbook register is the difference between financial life verses death." Despite this reality, many people do not take the time to balance their checkbook, and it is costing us billions of dollars.

I read an article titled "Rising Bank Fees Hit Consumers," published in USA Today by Kathy Chu. It reported banks, thrifts and credit unions collected a record $37.8 billion in service charges on accounts last year. This article also stated consumers paid about $10 billion in overdraft loans.[2] Just say, "Ouch," with me. The banking industry is making billions of dollars off consumers who do not take time to balance their checkbooks to know exactly what is in their accounts.

I want to say to the walking calculators, "It is impossible for you to remember every outstanding transaction, especially when you can barely remember where you put your keys." I beg you to take one minute to write down your transactions. All it takes is one missed outstanding transaction, and it can cost you hundreds of dollars in overdraft fees.

You know I have to stop and fuss for a minute. There is not a logical reason why we cannot be more responsible with our finances. It only takes one or two minutes to record a transaction. I promise if you would do this daily, it will save you a lot of headaches. If doing this daily is too much for you, then at least do it once a week. However, this might be too late.

I remember the first and only time I bounced a check. It was a penny error, and I had money in my savings account. You would think the bank would have at least paid the check for me or took the penny out of my savings account; instead bank policy was designed to take $30.00. Fortunately, I check my account daily and caught the error. I wanted to scream when I found out my account balance was a negative $30.01. However, I was able to transfer money from my savings to my checking account before any more damage was done. This goes to show your banks do not care anything about customer relationship; it is about the money. Please educate yourself about your financial institution's bank and service charges. Proverbs 29:18 states, "People perish for the lack of knowledge." The moral of this story is: One man's financial error is another man's gain.

I used to work part-time at a bank answering telephone calls from people checking on their account. About ninety-five percent (95%) of the calls were about the person's account being in overdraft. Typically, the account was overdrawn by hundreds, and sometimes thousands of dollars. My heart would go out to the customers, especially the elderly. Most of the time, the elderly customer would say, "The other bank would just pay these checks for me without a charge and notify me when my account was overdrawn." The other banks were family banks acquired by the bank I worked for. You can see why the family banks were acquired or out of business.

When we are irresponsible with our finances, it not only affects us, but it also affects others. It creates a domino effect. When we do not pay what we owe, it can make the other person unable to pay their bills. It can also cause the other person to pay their bills late, or they have to use their savings, until you do pay. Many times when we refuse to pay a person, we use excuses like, they are not hurting because they got money, or they can't suck blood from a turnip. This is unfair to the person because they were relying on you to make good on the money borrowed.

People, we must have character and integrity in our financial lives. We wouldn't want to work forty hours a week and someone give us a check that isn't good, so why do we do this to others. The word says, "Let everything be done decently and in order (1 Corinthians 14:40, NKJV)." This includes your financial affairs. Please balance your checkbook and pay others on time, after all, your financial life depends on it. Plus it will make life easier for those who may have to take care of your financial matters if something happens to you.

One of my friend's parents suddenly went home to be with the Lord. He was responsible for taking care of one of his family member's finances who was in a nursing home. His family wanted control over his finances. My friend had to quickly get things together and turn them over to an attorney. If her father had not been as detail as he was with the checkbook registers, it would have been a mess trying to put things together. Based on the information provided in the checkbooks, I was able to put together several financial reports for her. The attorney stated, "He was impressed with how professional everything was presented and the financial detail provided." Please, please, please, get your finances in order because it is costing you thousands of dollars, and you never know what will happen.

ENDNOTES

1. DNA Forensics (2009, June 16), Human Genome Projection Information. Retrieved from http://www.ornl.gov/hgmis/elsi/forensics.shtml.

2. Chu, Kathy (2005, October 4). Rising Bank Fees Hit Consumers. USA Today. Retrieved from http://www.usatoday.com/money/industries/banking/2005-10-04-bank-fees-usat_x.htm.

EXERCISE – CHAPTER 12

1. Pull out your checkbook and look at the transactions you have made over the last month, what is your checkbook saying to you and the treasures of your heart? What do you need to change?

   _____
   _____
   _____

2. Over the last year, how much have you spent on overdraft or bank fees? How much are you wasting on overdraft protection that could go towards helping someone else or getting out of debt?

   _____
   _____
   _____
   _____
   _____

3. This exercise is going to be a little hard, but I want you to think about a situation where you did not have financial character or integrity. Example, you borrowed money from someone and did not pay them back. Repent and ask the Lord how He wants you to make that situation right?

   _____
   _____
   _____
   _____
   _____

PRAYER AND DECLARATION

Dear Father God, Your Word says to let all things be done in decency and in order, so I am asking You to help me to become responsible with my financial matters. Father, reveal to me the financial plan that You have for my life. Give me the strategies that I need to be successful, and I promise to follow them line upon line, precept upon precept.

When I am confused, stressed or frustrated, bring forth Your peace and passion to accomplish the financial race that has been set before me. Let me feel Your overwhelming love for me to make provisions where there seems to be none.

Father help me to become focused and disciplined with my finances and begin to connect me with those who will hold me accountable and support me in the vision that You are setting for my life. Father, help me to set order in my life and to begin to do the things that I know to do like balancing my checkbook and budgeting for the things that I need as well as desire. When I am anxious, help me to be patient and to wait on You because there is a time and a season for every activity under the sun.

I decree and declare over my life that I am a disciple of Christ in every area of my life, including my finances. I am a lamp that sits on a hill and will never be hidden, but I will shine the glory of God in my finances by being a good steward and doing things in an orderly manner. When I don't know what to do, I will be like the king and search the heart of God concerning every financial transaction. I am like a well-watered garden and I will not experience drought, lack or brokenness as I follow the will of the Lord for it is impossible for Him to lie. I decree and declare I will not only be financially responsible, but I will have financial character and integrity. I will pay Caesar and anyone else that I owe on time and when I can't I will make arrangements, without guilt, shame or avoidance. I am more than a conqueror and I can do all things through Christ who strengthens me. AMEN.

PART SEVEN

ESTABLISHING A SAVINGS ACCOUNT

Chapter Thirteen

ALL SEASON FINANCES

Ecclesiastes 3:1 *- "To everything there is a season, a time for every purpose under the heaven (NKJV)."*

I am a native of Tennessean. Tennessee used to be known for experiencing all four seasons, winter, spring, summer, and fall. Winters were cold and snow was guaranteed, spring brought forth the rain, blooming flowers and high pollen, the summers were hot with birds and bugs flying everywhere, and as fall approached, the leaves were sure to change and the air was crisp and fresh. In these days and times there is no longer a clear distinction between the seasons. Example, in October 2007, we experienced a Red October, this is when we experienced ninety-degree weather, which resulted in a Christmas tree shortage due to the dry weather.

Just like the earth, our finances have the ability to go from season to season and sometimes it can even cross seasons. You can have a financial summer in the midst of an economic winter, but

Kingdom Finances for Kingdom Building

the key to how you survive each season depends on your preparation, as well as, your perception.

Imagine this simple little illustration: One who has a coat, gloves, boots and hats can survive the cold of winter better than one who does not. The difference is preparation. No matter what the reasons are, the person without will have a tough winter and their perception will be distorted. The person who has the winter items will breeze through winter and their perception will be quite different.

EXERCISE – CHAPTER 13

1. Identify your financial season.
   _____
   _____
   _____

2. Take a financial inventory. Have you planned and prepared for a sudden change in your financial season? If not what is holding you back?
   _____
   _____
   _____

3. What financial garments are you missing to prepare for the seasons that may come your way? Your financial garments are insurance, savings, retirement, wills, etc.
   _____
   _____
   _____

PRAYER AND DECLARATION

Dear Father God, help me to be a good steward and to be prepared for whatever season that comes financially. I realize this world is forever changing, but You are the one constant in my life. You are the same today, yesterday and forevermore. You are the God who knows all and sees all, so I thank You for walking with me, leading me and guiding me in whatever financial season I am experiencing. However, I want to be conscious of what season I am in and how to be ready to transition from one season to another without financially dying. Give me the wisdom, revelation and knowledge of the five virgins who were prepared for the bridegroom's arrival with oil burning in their lamps. Make me like the sons of Issachar who knew the times and the seasons. Help me to be sensitive to Your spirit in regards to the finances that have been placed in my possession to glorify your kingdom.

I decree and declare over my life that I will be ready in season and out of season for whatever financial season that comes my way in and through Christ Jesus. I will be as gentle as a dove and as wise as a serpent when it comes to financial transactions and strategies because I have the Holy Spirit within me, leading and guiding me into all truth. I will not be anxious for anything, but I will take every financial matter to the Lord in prayer and supplication because He is all knowing and sees far ahead of me. I am an obedient and submitted servant to the Lord; therefore, I can never go wrong following the Lord's will for my life financially. I am like a well-watered garden that will never dry out. And when I go astray, I trust the Lord to make my crooked paths straight without worry, fear or dread. AMEN

Chapter Fourteen

WHO MOVED THE CHEESE
❦

"**Proverbs 25:2** – *"It is the glory of God to conceal a matter, but the glory of kings is to search out a matter (NKJV)."*

I am a Christian, so I believe there are two perspectives to every situation. There is a natural perspective and a spiritual perspective. The natural perspective is the perspective that considers those things, situations and circumstances that we can see with our natural, physical eyes. The spiritual perspective is the perspective that considers those things, situations and circumstances that are actually happening in the heavens on your behalf. These are the things we cannot see with our natural eyes. As a result, we must go before the Lord to petition, inquire and reason things out with Him (Isaiah 1:18). These are the things we hope for and must bring into manifestation through the living, breathing and creative word of God. The word tells us to speak those things that are not as though they were (Romans 4:17). Often times we label our situation and circumstance from our natural perspective, but if we take the time to see things from a spiritual perspective, we will find out that things are actually contrary to what we see. Now I am not saying live in a fantasy world, but I am asking you to seek the Lord to find out His perspective on your financial circumstance and situation. His word is the truth no matter what your natural situation is telling you. Our duty is to grab hold of what He is saying and to believe by faith that it is a done deal. Your next step is to work your faith. We are to be doers of the word and not just hearers of the word (James 1:22, NKJV). If you are experiencing a financial winter, then there are things you will have to do to collaborate and partner with the Lord to turn things around. Again, God does not work in magic, but He does perform miracles and He does partner with us to accomplish things upon the earth.

If you feel the urgency to begin to save money like never before, then that is God preparing you for a season ahead that you might not know. Here's my testimony. In 2010 my career took a route that I was not expecting, but years prior God laid upon my heart to begin saving at least a year of my household expenses. I couldn't tell you why I was doing this at the time, but I began the mission and He made the way for me to accomplish the goal through a promotion, which would ultimately result in me leaving the place of employment I had known for nine years. It was because I was obedient to the Holy Spirit that I was able to have a financial summer in the midst of what should have been a financial winter. I was able to live off the harvest and the fruit of the abundance that was stored away for such a time as this. I also had the awesome opportunity to visit the Holy Land, Israel, and rest in peace, knowing all my bills were paid on time. Who does this when they are unemployed? Only the Lord could have done such a miraculous thing.

In the beginning, this felt like a financial winter for me, despite the fact that I had at least a year's savings to cover my household expenditures. This occurred because I did not have God's perspective on the matter I only looked at what was going on in the natural. Eventually, I got my peace about the situation and began to forgive, it was then that things became clearer; God was launching me out into new waters to start my own business, as well as, giving me the opportunity to go on a journey to Israel and to get some much needed rest from years of work. I am sure He is doing much more, but it all has not manifested to my natural eyes yet, but the lesson is to seek the Lord to find out what He is doing, then you can partner with Him and come into agreement with the heavens on your behalf.

Remember, with the Lord, one day is as a thousand years, and a thousand years is as one day (2 Peter 3:8, NKJV). Just like that you can go from one season to the next. It is like hitting the lottery. One day you are at the lowest point you think you ever had, but within the next minute you find out you hit the lottery. And you begin to praise the Lord because you knew one series of events was crucial to the next series of events, meaning it took the financial winter to usher you into your financial summer. No matter what the situation, all things will work together for your good (Romans 8:28). If you don't believe me, then read the story about Joseph in Genesis 37.

Joseph went from the pit to the palace; from the palace to prison; from prison to Chief Administrator over Egypt. Everything we go through has a purpose, but we have to seek the Lord to see what He is saying about the matter. He loves for us to run after Him. He tells us in Matthew 7:7, "Ask, and it will be given to you; seek, and you will find; knock, and it will be opened to you." Jeremiah 33:3, says, "Call to Me and I will answer you and tell you great and unsearchable things you do not know."

Also don't curse your financial winter because it could be truly a blessing in disguise. Learn whatever lessons you need to learn and let the Lord guide you through in His peace, rest and joy. Psalms 23:1-3, says, "The Lord is my shepherd; I shall not want. He makes me to lie down in green pastures; He leads me beside the still waters. He restores my soul; He leads me in the paths of righteousness for His name's sake." Anywhere God is leading you He will protect you, teach you, provide for you, cleanse you and cover you, even if it is in the wilderness place. It is in the wilderness that we learn to rely on the God for everything we need because life as we know it has dried up, but the voice of the Lord will lead us to places of provision.

To bring this point home with a biblical example, let's look at the Israelites. God began to dry up everything they were dependent upon for their survival while they were in Egypt. They were used to Pharaoh providing them with everything they needed. Who would have thought the hardest season of their life was only preparation for what they would experience in their journey to the promise land. Except this time, instead of relying upon man and themselves, they would have to rely upon God.

In Exodus, Chapter 5, Pharaoh commanded the taskmasters not to provide them with brick or straw to complete their quotas, in addition to more work laid upon the men. Even if the Israelites did not acknowledge who was helping them during their time of trouble, we know it was only God who could provide them with the straw and bricks to complete their quotas. They were mad at Moses and Aaron for doing this to them, but God allowed it to build their reliance upon Him. It was part of God's plan for their lives. He knew they would need to rely on Him to survive the wilderness and get to the promise land.

Throughout this season of preparation, God kept testing the Israelites' dependency upon Him. They had to trust His presence in the pillar of cloud to lead them during the day and the pillar of fire to give them light during the night. In the wilderness, they had to rely on God to provide them with manna, quail and water, as well as, maintain their clothing daily. However, it was their murmuring and complaining that kept them in the wilderness for forty years and eventually led to their death.

We have to be cautious not to be like the Israelites when we are in a financial wilderness or winter because it can lead us to a financial death or bankruptcy. As a result, we find ourselves on a financial merry-go-round that plays out like a never-ending story because we will not die to our flesh and listen to what the Spirit is trying to tell us about our financial situation. Instead, we continue to rely on credit cards, jobs or our way of doing things, instead of relying upon God's way of doing things. We won't tithe, make a budget or cut up the credit cards, so sometimes God will bring a financial storm or financial winter to shake us into giving up what we thought was stable.

Hebrews 12:25-27 says, "See that you do not refuse Him who speaks. For if they did not escape who refused Him who spoke on earth, much more shall we not escape if we turn away from Him who speaks from heaven, whose voice then shook the earth; but now He has promised, saying, "Yet once more I shake not only the earth, but also heaven." Now this, "Yet once more," indicates the removal of those things that are being shaken, as of things that are made, that the things which cannot be shaken may remain (NIV)." When we are hard headed, we turn a three-day journey into forty years.

Kingdom Finances for Kingdom Building

EXERCISE – CHAPTER 14

1. What perspective are you looking at your financial situation? Have you sought the Lord on His point of view?

   _____
   _____
   _____
   _____

2. What is the last thing the Lord told you to do financially that you have not done? Begin to partner with God on that thing and pray for His guidance. Find out what your part is.

   _____
   _____
   _____
   _____

3. Reflect on a time when you were in a financial situations where you seen the Lord's hand move or a time when you followed the leading of the Lord to do something financially and it prepared you for something that was ahead of you?

   _____
   _____
   _____
   _____

PRAYER AND DECLARATION

Dear Father God, my desire is to seek You and find out Your good, perfect and acceptable will for my life financially. You know the plans for my life, plans to prosper me, not to harm me, but to give me a hope and a future. And when I cry out to You, You will show me great and mighty things that I do not know. Help me Father not to live by fear, doubt and dread, but to live by faith, soundness of mind and boldness according to Your Word. Your Word is a lamp unto my feet and light unto my path. Therefore, I trust You to make the crooked places straight in my life.

Show up in my finances as I am obedient to Your will, way and purpose for my life. Lord, be my Financial Advisor and show me the Financial Plan that will bring You glory in the earth. Help me to rest and trust You no matter what season I am in financially and to be prepared for those seasons. You said in Your Word, Your people perish for the lack of knowledge and vision. Help me write the vision and make it plan so that I can see it, as well as others and run with it. I know it will tarry, but it shall come to pass in my life. Show me the way I should go and I will not lean to my own understanding. Bestow upon me, Your spirit of wisdom, understanding, counsel, might, knowledge and fear of You in every financial transaction and activity.

I decree and declare over my life that I am abounding in love and in faith. I am growing in wisdom and in stature and in favor with God and man. Holy Spirit, I am in partnership with You, so remind me of the things the Lord has spoken and I will be quick to be obedient to follow for You do not lie or speak on Your own authority. I will prosper financially and be successful because the Lord Almighty is with me in every endeavor and has destined me to do great exploits for His kingdom. I am the head and not the tail; I am a lender, not a borrower. Every need is met with nothing missing, lacking or broken. I am born to be a blessing to others and to serve You, Father, with all my mind, body, spirit and soul. AMEN

Chapter Fifteen

GET UP, PICK UP AND WALK

John 5:8, 14 - *"Get up! Pick up your mat and walk." "Stop sinning or something worse may happen to you (NIV)."*

In Chapter Fourteen, *Who Moved the Cheese*, I gave us a little break, but many times our financial winter is due to us and our sin. Therefore, our perspective is like the one without the coat, gloves and hat in the wintertime. We didn't prepare for the winter because it was summer and everything was lovely. I had to get my toes, nails and hair done. I had to get the nice ride with the rims and the booming system. I needed that big screen television and that video game. And let's not forget the overdue vacation that I didn't have the money to go on, so I charged it. And who goes on a vacation without new outfits. Yeah! Yeah! The list goes on and on.

Then we loose our job or an emergency comes along that sends us on the financial merry-go-round because we didn't prepare for the storm. Trust me; I have been here in my own life. If we are not careful with doing things in our own strength and will, we can end up in financial bondage. This is when we cannot see our way out and we continue down a road of destruction because we become blind and deaf to the voice of the Lord regarding that area. We become content and it becomes a way of life. Now the very thing that we were to have dominion over controls us.

Believe it or not, this is idolatry because we are serving other gods in our lives and making sacrifices unto them. God hates sin and He is jealous for us (2 Corinthians 11:2). We must repent and turn away from those things that are not pleasing in His sight. He is a gracious and merciful God. He has the power to set us free but we must be willing to invite Him in. When He sets you free, you are free indeed, so move by faith and ask the Lord to help you in the areas that are keeping you in financial bondage. Choose to let go of the insecurities, self-worthlessness and hopelessness. It was true when the group En Vogue song, "Free your mind and the rest will follow."

Romans 6:23 could not have said it better, "The wages of sin is death, but the gift of God is eternal life." We get to live life and life more abundantly when we choose to follow after Christ Jesus. Doing things our own way will kill us and lead us into financial death and destruction. It is sin to rely on our on strength, credit cards, and jobs to meet our needs. It is idolatry. We have to make a choice to free our minds, renew our minds with the word of the Lord. Trust in the Lord and do good; dwell in the land and feed on His faithfulness. We are told to delight ourselves in the Lord, and He will give us the desires of our heart (Psalm 37:3-4). Jesus warns the man in John 5:8-14, to stop sinning or a worse thing would come upon him. Notice when God speaks this verse to the man, it is a command, not something he asks the man to do.

Get up! Picking up your mat and walking is not making excuses for your financial situation, but assuming responsibility. It is making a choice to do what you can do in the natural like building a budget; saving, getting rid of the credit cards and making other necessary sacrifices the Spirit of the Lord leads you to make. The spiritual things are to become a giver of tithes, offering and seed into the kingdom, as well as, other spiritual things the Spirit of the Lord may lead you to do, like getting rid of some clutter in your house and giving it to charity. It is beginning to take authority over those things that have been carrying you, instead of you carrying them. The man had an infirmity for thirty-eight years because he was relying on man to do something he could have done for himself. But in one encounter with Jesus, he was healed and delivered, and so can your finances (Read John 5).

I pray that you will have an encounter with God that will change your financial destiny. I pray for Him to speak to you in dreams and visions, circumstances and situations. I pray for a new order of doing things financially that will bless the kingdom and change generations to come in your family. "It is a new day, a new way and a new time. Your latter days will be better than your former days, but you must Get Up! Pick up your mat and walk. And sin no more." God is faithful - just trust Him.

EXERCISE – CHAPTER 15

1. What is it that has you in financial bondage? What have you given authority over you that you should have authority over? Dig deep and get to the root of the problem by asking yourself what, when, why and how long I have had this issue. An example could be fear being rejected.

   _____
   _____
   _____
   _____

2. Look around your house and find things to let go of to be a blessing to someone else. Also ask the Lord what He wants you to let go of that is keeping you financially bound.

   _____
   _____
   _____
   _____

3. Take sometime to reflect on things you have done to put and keep you in financial bondage. Repent and ask the Lord for the strategy to break free.

   _____
   _____
   _____
   _____

PRAYER AND DECLARATION

Dear Father God, help me to be sensitive to the leading of Your Spirit. Let me not do things in my own strength or power, but by the Spirit of the Lord. Father, I want to serve You with my whole heart, mind and soul. I promise not to serve any other god because You are the one and only True Living God. Thank You for snatching me out of the miry clay and setting my feet upon the rock. Father, show me the sin that is in my life that is leading me to a spiritual as well as a financial death. Help me to break free from the things that are keeping me bound. You came to set the captives free and open the prison doors. Heal my broken heart; give me a garment of praise and beauty for my ashes. Transition me from this place of rebellion, bondage and death to a place that is obedient, free and exuding with life financially. God I want to be in the wealthy place seated by rivers of living waters. I know with You I am free indeed.

I decree and declare over my life that I will no longer wait or depend on man to do what I can do for myself. I will arise and shine from my place of sin and press forward to the prize of the high calling with all resilience and tenacity to live the financial life You desire for my life. I realize I have sinned against You and only You. I repent and turn away from everything that is not of You and I set my mind, soul and body to search for the deeper things of Your Spirit. God I cannot fail with You. You are the Way, the Truth and the Life. Help me to soar on wings as an eagle and not grow weary in the race that is set before me. I am victorious in You, Christ Jesus. I can and will overcome financial bondage by the blood of the Lamb and the word of my testimony. I can and will do all things through You who strengthen me. AMEN

Chapter Sixteen

GOLIATH MUST DIE

1 Samuel 17:46 -"This day the LORD will deliver you into my hand, and I will strike you and take your head from you (NKJV)."

It is never too late to come out of financial bondage. You can do all things through Christ who strengthens you. However, your mind must be renewed and your perception must be changed to think kingdom thoughts. This means you must get to the root of the matter and decapitate the giant that has been driving your financial decisions. Getting to the root of the matter is to dig deep and to go where no man has gone before within you. Whatever it is, ask the Lord to reveal it so you can conquer it and move forward in freedom and liberty.

Are you making bad financial decisions because of unresolved childhood issues? Are you trying to prove something to people who have hurt you in your past? What is the driving force that has led you into financial bondage?

In 1 Samuel 17, when David was fighting Goliath, he prevailed over him with a sling and a stone, but he silenced the Philistine (the enemy) forever when he cut the head of Goliath off. And the men of Israel and Judah were able to conquer the very thing that was conquering them. They were able to plunder the enemy's tents, instead of the enemy plundering their tents. Remember, "We wrestle not against flesh and blood but principalities, against powers, against rulers of darkness of this age, against spiritual hosts of wickedness in the heavenly places (Ephesians 6:12, NKJV)." Refusing to face the giant will destroy you and cause you much grief and pain, it will make you a slave to those things that you are to have dominion and control over. Dare to go there, even if your enemy is you. Once you have decapitated your Goliath, then you can take the plunder of the tents and start afresh.

The story of David teaches the valuable lesson of not only facing the giants in our lives, but defeating them once and for all. The Word of the Lord promises that our enemies might come in one way, but they will have to flee seven ways (Deuteronomy 28:7). Once we decapitate our Goliaths, we are able to operate in the power and authority that God has placed on the inside of us. It is then we are able to see what we have not seen before, do what we were not able to do before, and think like we were not able to think before. We will be free from the mentality and perception that kept us in bondage.

Changing your perception and mind set is being like the servant when Elijah kept sending him back to look for the sign of the abundance of rain (1 Kings 18:41-46). The servant had to go back seven times before he saw a cloud as small as a man's hand rising out of the sea. Again, I am not promising you some fly by night debt free plan. But what I am promising you is if you do what you can do; God will do what He can do. Many times, we do not want to hear this. We want a hocus pocus miracle to happen, and it is not going to happen like that. When God wanted to do something in the land, He spoke to man and used him to get the assignment done because He gave him dominion and authority in this earth at the beginning of time. Please get to the root of your issues with the Lord, so you can walk in freedom and liberty in every area of your life.

I leave you with this wisdom: The purpose of your Goliath is to make you doubt our Lord and Savior Jesus Christ. His aim to steal, kill and destroy (John 10:10), and he begins the process with his words. Remember it was words and dialect that satan used to get Eve out of the Lords will. It will be the words of Goliath that will come to make you hopeless and doubtful about this process to freedom. Most of the time he will use those who are closest to you, but remember the word of the Lord will shut the enemy's mouth.

Bondage is dangerous because it can make you think you can't ever get free, which leads to hopelessness, so you learn to dwell comfortably into something you were not designed to live in. Bondage is a lie from the pit of hell - so don't believe the hype. The truth is God came to give you life and life more abundantly. Now that is freedom and freedom is everything. I dare not leave without telling you that freedom will cost you some things and some people. You will walk away from some and some will walk away from you, but know with all of your heart, the price is worth paying. Believe you deserve it, be willing to fight for it and God will back you up.

EXERCISE – CHAPTER 16

1. What is your Goliath? Be honest and put a name to it. How is it intimidating you and torturing you or have you become a friend of your Goliath?

   _____
   _____
   _____
   _____

2. What weapons as the Lord placed in your hands to defeat Goliath that you are not using? Faith without works is dead.

   _____
   _____
   _____

3. Name three benefits of decapitating the Goliath of your life?

   _____
   _____
   _____
   _____

PRAYER AND DECLARATION

Dear Father God, I have been dwelling in a land that you did not prepare for me, a land that is dry and sucking the life out of me; it is the land of bondage. This land brings me no joy, peace or rest, but only breeds discouragement, restlessness, hopelessness and complacency. As I begin to evaluate my situation, I am not living, but only existing.

Father, You came to set the captives free, so open up the prison walls for me, give me beauty for my ashes, the oil of gladness for mourning, and the garment of praise instead of despair. Father, deliver the enemy into my hand today, so I can strike him and take his head off once and for all. I want my freedom and I deserve my freedom. Freedom is everything and I am willing to fight for it no matter the cost. Your joy is my strength and You will back me up. If You are with me and for me, then whom shall I fear.

Father, You said in your Word, "Now faith is the substance of things hoped for and the evidence of things not seen." This means I have to have a now faith and that starts today. Today, I make a conscious decision to make friends with freedom and break all ties with bondage. I loose the shackles from my mouth, hands and feet to praise the Lord and make war against the enemy. I will trust in the Lord with all of my heart and I will not lean to my own understanding, but I will have the faith to only believe what the Lord has spoken. Therefore, I am crossing over into my land flowing with milk and honey. I walk into my destiny with the fire and anointing of the Lord upon me. It is His fire that will consume that which is not of Him. It is His anointing that will break the yokes.

I decree and declare over my life that it will never be the same because I have been redeemed by the blood of the Lamb and my Father loves me. Goliath, you are a defeated foe. You have no rule or reign over my life anymore because the Father has set me free. Today, I kill you with the Word of the Lord and I choose life and life more abundantly. Now I am free. AMEN

Chapter Seventeen

THE ANT MENTALITY

Proverbs 6:8 – *"The ant stores its provision in summer and gathers its food at harvest (NIV)."*

Last but not least, if your finances are going to survive all seasons, you have to have an ant mentality. Yes, God will use the foolish things of the world to shame the wise (1 Corinthians 1:27). Who would have thought a little old ant could teach us a financial lesson about storing up provision in the summer to gather food at harvest? The two key words of this wisdom scripture that grabs my attention are provision and gather. I took the liberty of looking up both definitions in the American Heritage College Dictionary. "Provision" means the act of preparatory action or measure; a stock of necessary supplies. "Gather" means a collection or an accumulation; to grow or increase by degrees.[1] My financial definition of the ant mentality is when one takes the necessary preparatory actions to stock, store up, invest and save funding they can reap benefits from during a particular financial season. The awesome thing is what you put up today will carry you through tomorrow. Better yet, it will be your financial coat in a financial winter. With the right clothing on for the season, it sure feels cozy and warm, especially with some hot cocoa, which is the extra or interest.

ENDNOTES

1. *The American Heritage Dictionary*, Third Edition. Boston: Houghton Mifflin Company, 1993, pp. 1102 & 563.

PART EIGHT

WISDOM AND ENCOURAGEMENT

Chapter Eighteen

WISDOM OF MY MOTHER

Psalms 37:30-31 *–"The mouth of the righteous speaks wisdom, and his tongue talks of justice. The law of his God is in his heart. None of his steps shall slide (NKJV)."*

One day a friend and I were sitting in the living room talking with my mother, who I just adore. She is truly a woman of great wisdom. She thinks I don't listen to her half the time, but I really do. Anyway, she began to tell us, our generation doesn't know what it is like to be in a recession, or not to have, just like her generation doesn't know what it is like to experience a depression. Then she makes the most profound statement that arrested my spirit, "What can be a recession for some, can be a depression for others."

She began to tell us her experience during the 1975 recession. Mother had been working on a job where she was not happy. During those times, African Americans were reminded they were the first to do anything. Mother was the first African American to progress in her company from a mail carrier to a sales secretary, and her coworkers never let her forget it. Mother got tired of the bureaucracy, so she decided to resign from her job. Plus her strained relationship with her boss and the fact that my brother was in the first grade and no one would be at home when he got out of school made it even easier for her to resign.

Mother decided she would stay until her company found another African American to fill the position. Things were done by quotas back then, and her position was earmarked for an African American person. It was on a Monday morning when the company found someone to fill the position. This is when the story moves pretty fast. On Monday, mother was out of work and by Wednesday, daddy received a pink slip and on Friday, he was out of work. To add fuel to the fire, they just purchased a new house and furniture, plus had two babies to take care of all on $127.00 per week in unemployment money. Who can live off of that?

Now I know why my mother said it was a depression for them, in the midst of a recession. As I stated above, there was not any preparation for what was coming ahead. I love my parents, but like many of us today, they didn't have the ant mentality. We just think the sun is going to shine always, so we don't prepare for the rain, or we have the mentality I will conquer that giant when I get there. Lord, please have mercy upon us.

God was faithful to them during this season of their life, despite their lack of preparation. Their unemployment checks always came in the mail on time, and God provided when they did not have. When this season was over for them, God sent an angel to meet my mother at the unemployment office to give her a job. So again, look at this from both a spiritual and natural perspective, and don't allow a recession to be a depression in your life.

I challenge you to get out of the debt you are in during this season. This economy is unstable, and the sun is not guaranteed to shine always. We as a people must start thinking about the future, and we must start somewhere. I don't care if you don't have anything but two extra dollars, use it to get out of debt and find a way to save something. Ask the Lord for a plan, I promise He will give it to you. He said, "If any man lacks wisdom, He should ask God, who gives generously to all without finding fault, and it will be given to him (James 1:5)." There is one thing I am learning as we speak to obey is better than sacrifice (1 Samuel 15:22).

Chapter Nineteen

JUST A LITTLE ENCOURAGEMENT

Ecclesiastes 7:8 *– "The end of a matter is better than its beginning, and patience is better than pride. (NIV)"*

I started my debt free plan years ago. Sometimes, I had to work a second job to do it, but I was at the point of "by any means necessary." Somewhere in the process, I lost my way, but a word came to me from the Lord to get back on track. It was as if God was warning me, "The days of Joseph shall come again. There will be seven years of prosperity, which is the season to save and store up for the seven years of famine (Genesis 41:29-30)." Well, I got serious and began to pray to the Lord for a plan. I didn't know how I was going to accomplish all the things the Lord had placed upon my heart to accomplish financially in three years, but I can say, "My obedience to Christ has paid off, and He has been faithful throughout the process.

I have honestly seen God's miraculous work in my finances. I promise at one point, it seemed like He turned water into wine (John 2:1-11)."

Here's my testimony in detail. I set a goal of how many bills I wanted to get paid off before January 1, 2006, and how much I would need to pay extra to meet this goal. I began cutting things out of my budget like eating out for lunch and going to the vending machines, along with other things. I have to be honest and tell you, I got off track sometimes, but overall, I remained focused. For the most part, getting out of debt is a mental thing because there is nothing like putting hundreds of dollars extra on a credit card, student loan or car payment, especially when you can think of a million other things you want to do with that money. But I had to realize, the sacrifice I was making for the next three years of my life would pay off dearly and set me up for something awesome. Getting off track delayed a couple of bills from getting paid off on the date I set. I got back on track, and I am proud to say that I have paid off my last student loan in February 2009. It took ten years from graduation to do it, but it is finished. Hallelujah, praise the Lord.

Just think, most people tell you to be content with paying student loans or stretching out a mortgage for thirty years, but the devil is a liar. We can truly own things and pay them off. We do not have to sit back and allow others to get rich off of us. Based upon my budget, I will be officially debt free February 2008, and I praise the Lord in advance. My next financial goal is to see a house paid for in my lifetime and I want to be the first to do it in my family. Is it a struggle?

Yes. Do you have to give up things? Yes, but there is nothing like the day, you pay off a bill. It liberates you because that is one less person you are enslaved to.

I want the life God came to give me, life and life more abundantly (John 10:10). If people in the world are paying off their bills and living debt free, then surely we as Christians can do the same because we know the One who owns the world and the fullness thereof. He owns cattle on a thousand hills (Psalm 50:10). He said we are the head, not the tail; above only, not beneath. I am a lender and not a borrower (Deuteronomy 28:13, NKJV). So, today I am taking back my inheritance in Jesus Name for whom the Son sets free is free indeed (John 8:36). And I declare, "We will owe no man anything, but love (Romans 13:8)."

FINAL REMARKS

I pray this book blessed you as much as it has blessed me. When God gave me this assignment, I did not think I could complete it. I often asked God, "Why would you have me to write something that I have not overcome yet." His reply was, "You will walk this one out with the people." God's thoughts are not our thoughts, and His ways are not our ways (Isaiah 55:9). And right now I am totally at awe with Him because I have completed an assignment that I know I could not have done in my own natural strength. The point I am making is, if I could write this book, then you can get out of debt, but it must all be done with the Spirit of the Lord. Just like this book took great sacrifice, so will getting out of debt, but if you keep moving and stay focused, you will see the sunshine at the end of the tunnel.

God has taught and revealed so many awesome things to me, while writing this book. He continues to show Himself mighty and strong in my life, as well as, in my finances. I know I will be debt free because I see the vision, embrace the vision and work the vision God has given me. Do I get off course sometimes? Yes, but God is so gracious and merciful to get me back on course and He will do the same for you. However, you have to take the initiative and do what you can do. Dedicate what you have over to the Lord and watch Him multiply it in your life. Make the sacrifices, even when it is hard because it will be worth it in the long run. Ecclesiastes 7:8 says, "The ending of a matter is better than the beginning of a matter."

I know my ending, which is my future is so much brighter than my beginning and so is yours. Forget the past, leave it behind you and press towards the prize of the higher calling by looking to the Author and Finisher of your faith (Philippians 3:14 & Hebrews 12:2, KJV). He is able to complete the very work He began in you (Philippians 1:6, NKJV). He already knows the ending of your chapter in your book of life. There is nothing that is too impossible for Him to handle in your life and there is nothing He does not see (Luke 1:37). Jesus loves you. He wants absolutely nothing but the best for you and your offspring. I promise you, if you walk with Him, He will walk with you.

Call unto Him for He will show you great and mighty things, which you do not know (Jeremiah 33:3, NASB), but you have to trust Him, believe Him and rest in Him. I have never seen the righteous forsaken, nor His seed begging for bread (Psalms 37:25, KJV). He owns cattle on a thousand hills (Psalm 50:10). He is seated at the right hand of the Father in heaven, making intercessions for you (Romans 3:34). He is an heir to the kingdom and so are you, so walk in the dominion, power and authority He has given you to take back everything the enemy has stolen from you, as well as the things you surrendered to him.

I am called to bring the good news. So I leave you with this good news, you do not have to stay where you are. Things can change and will change because there is a new sheriff in town and His name is Jesus. He is able to do exceedingly, abundantly, above and beyond what you can ever think or even imagine according to the power that is within you (Romans 3:20, NKJV). You are on the brink of something new that has never been done before in your life. You are about to see the dawning of a new day in your life, financially, physically, mentally and emotionally because it is all about His kingdom.

Blessings and Love
Kellie L.

Request for information, conferences, speaking engagements, or small group teachings should be addressed to:

Kellie L. Morgan
www.kingdomfinances40@yahoo.com

Also follow me on tumblr.com

www.anointeddove.tumblr.com